# THE DEVIL'S GREATEST FEAR

Through scriptural insights, this book explores how identity is central to the spiritual battle—from the devil's schemes to erase names from the Book of Life to the chilling symbolism of hell as a place of lost identity. While reading, you will be challenged to reclaim your identity in Christ, dismantle the devil's lies spoken into your life, and walk in victory, knowing your name is written in heaven.

Jennifer is a dear friend of ours and a Spirit-filled and hungry minister of the gospel, and this book displays the results of her diligent study and prayer, born from her deep hunger for Jesus' righteousness and kingdom. In a day and age when the lack of identity is prevalent in this generation and across the nation, this book helps readers embrace what Jesus says about the believer—those whose names are written in the Book of Life! I pray this book greatly blesses you, helping you walk in your identity and cast off all lies and deceiving arrows of the enemy.

—STEVE KANG
FOUNDER, REVIVE THE NATIONS
EVANGELIST, ONNURI CHURCH

In a world where many hide behind titles, masks, and false identities, Jennifer Bagnaschi's book offers a powerful reminder of our true identity in Christ. Through the gripping stories of those who are searching for self-identity, Jennifer beautifully illustrates how superficial labels can deceive us, but only through a true encounter with Christ do we find our real purpose and destiny. This book is a compelling call to look beyond worldly titles and false identities and discover the lasting identity that the

Bible affirms. Our self-worth, calling, and future must be grounded in Jesus. I believe the biggest crisis facing Christians today is the "identity crisis." I often find that many people do not know that God wrote a book about their lives long before they were in their mother's womb. King David saw his "Book of Destiny" (Ps. 139), which caused him to do miraculous things. This book is a must-read for anyone searching to find their God-given destiny. Once a true believer finds who they really are, the authority they carry becomes evident. With this new revelation, miracles, signs, and wonders become daily events.

—Joe Kirkwood
Pastor, Cornerstone Outreach Ministries
Author, *Miracles Are Easy*

Jennifer Bagnaschi is a wonderful, powerful, and authentic minister of the gospel. This book is a timely, gripping, and soul-awakening message for a generation chasing validation in titles and achievements. Jennifer does a great job helping readers avoid the most common mistake of finding our worth in what we do (even what we do for Christ) instead of who we are in Him, and she shows how to do it in a practical way. This is the only way we can actually achieve our purpose.

—Freddy Ramirez
Host, *Heaven Come* TV Show
Founder, *Prophet* Magazine

JENNIFER BAGNASCHI

# THE
# DEVIL'S
# GREATEST
# FEAR

CHARISMA
HOUSE

THE DEVIL'S GREATEST FEAR by Jennifer Bagnaschi
Published by Charisma House, an imprint of Charisma Media
1150 Greenwood Blvd., Lake Mary, Florida 32746

Copyright © 2025 by Jennifer Bagnaschi. All rights reserved.

Unless otherwise noted, all Scripture quotations are from the New King James Version®. Copyright © 1982 by Thomas Nelson. Used by permission. All rights reserved.

Scripture quotations marked kjv are from the King James Version of the Bible.

While the author has made every effort to provide accurate, up-to-date source information at the time of publication, statistics and other data are constantly updated. Neither the publisher nor the author assumes any responsibility for errors or for changes that occur after publication. Further, the publisher and author do not have any control over and do not assume any responsibility for third-party websites or their content.

For more resources like this, visit MyCharismaShop.com and the author's website at deepbeliever.com.

Cataloging-in-Publication Data is on file with the Library of Congress.
International Standard Book Number: 978-1-63641-497-3
E-book ISBN: 978-1-63641-498-0

1 2025
Printed in the United States of America

Most Charisma Media products are available at special quantity discounts for bulk purchase for sales promotions, premiums, fund-raising, and educational needs. For details, call us at (407) 333-0600 or visit our website at charismamedia.com.

The word *satan* is lowercased throughout this book per the author's request.

*This book is dedicated to my other half: my hubby, Ed, who helps and supports me in everything I do. And to our two remarkable daughters, who never cease to amaze your father and me! You two set out to accomplish your dreams and goals, and you execute them! Everything we've taught you is in this book, so keep passing it through the generational line. I love you from the depths of my being.*

# CONTENTS

*Introduction* .................................. ix
1. Yeah...That Needs to Be Corrected ............ 1
2. Who Do You Think You Are?................ 13
3. Stop Chasing Titles and Start Living Your Purpose ..................................... 23
4. The Devil Has No Name .................... 39
5. The Devil Can't Give Names................. 57
6. No Souls in Hell.......................... 85
7. The Devil's Greatest Fear..................... 95
8. Fight! Fight! Fight!......................... 105
9. Don't Dance with the Devil................. 129
10. Gold in Your Pockets ...................... 145
11. Unlock the Supernatural .................... 157
12. What Are Angels Doing?................... 167
13. The Holy Spirit Gives You the Upper Hand.... 179
14. You're Kind of a Big Deal .................... 189

*A Personal Invitation from the Author*........ 205
*Notes* ...................................... 207
*About the Author*........................... 209

# INTRODUCTION

THE YEAR WAS 2004—just one year into my marriage. Life was exciting, unpredictable, and full of firsts. My husband and I had settled into a cozy basement apartment in Washington state, right in the heart of Silverdale. It wasn't a dark, musty place with creaky pipes; it was pretty nice. This place had arm lighting a good amount of space, and best of all it was ours. It felt like the perfect little spot for two newlyweds figuring out life together.

Then one day the phone rang. It was my mother, and the second I heard her voice I knew something was wrong.

"It's Nana," she said.

Now, let me pause here and tell you about Nana—my grandmother. She was a woman of faith, wisdom, and an unshakable love for butter pecan ice cream. And by that I mean *unshakable*. I have this vivid memory of walking downstairs in the middle of the night, the house completely dark. I flipped on the kitchen light and saw her sitting in the corner with a spoon in hand and a tub of butter pecan ice cream balanced on her lap like a priceless treasure.

"Nana, why are you eating ice cream in the dark?" I asked, trying not to laugh too hard.

She just gave me this look, as if I were the weird one for needing light to eat. And that was that. No explanation. Just Nana, her ice cream, and absolute peace.

So when my mother told me that Nana had stubbed her toe and the doctors were planning to amputate, it hit me hard. A stubbed toe? Amputation? How did we go from something that happens every day to something so permanent?

I called my dad and told him what was happening, still trying to process it. I muttered, "I guess it's the Lord's will."

But my dad stopped me cold.

"No," he said. "It's never the Lord's will for someone's body parts to be chopped off."

That was the moment I realized there are things in life that don't have to happen. There are battles that can be won before they even start, but many of us don't know how to fight them. We just assume that whatever happens must be God's plan.

But what if it's not?

What if the loss, the struggle, the suffering was never meant to be? What if the only reason we go through certain things is that we don't realize we have the power to stop them?

Nana's condition worsened. First they took her toes. Then they took her foot. Then part of her leg. And not long after, she passed away from complications. It was heartbreaking.

But the comfort in all this? I knew where she was. I knew she loved Jesus more than she loved butter pecan ice

*Introduction*

cream, and that's saying a lot. Now I picture her in heaven: sitting in a big, comfy chair, eating unlimited ice cream, walking on two perfect legs, and feeling no more pain.

But her situation left me thinking.

How many of us accept things we don't have to? How many of us live under constant attack, struggling, barely holding on—not because God wants it that way but because we don't know how to fight back?

I wrote this book because Christians should not be living as defeated as the unbelievers around us are. That's not what Jesus died for. Yet we've somehow been tricked into believing that powerless Christianity is the standard. It's not. The Bible is clear: We've been granted authority and given weapons, but many of us have no idea how to use them.

We're like someone who's been handed a sword but never told how to swing it, so we just sit there, getting beat up, thinking, "Well, maybe this is just my fate."

No. It's not.

The problem isn't that God hasn't equipped us to fight and win. The problem is that we don't know what we're doing with the equipment we've been given.

That's why I wrote this book—not just to teach you but to wake you up. If we, as the body of Christ, understood and walked in what we've been provided, the world wouldn't look as dark as it does right now.

So here's how this book works.

Every chapter starts with a story—sometimes funny, sometimes thought-provoking, but always something relatable to help you understand the deeper truth that follows. Think of it as a three-course meal:

- The appetizer: a short story to warm you up

- The entrée: the core of the chapter, where the meat is

- The dessert: the takeaway that leaves you full and satisfied, seeing your life with God differently than before

If parables worked for Jesus, I figured—hey, they might work for me too.

So grab a fork. Grab a spoon. (Or if you're like Nana, just grab a tub of ice cream and eat it in the dark. I won't judge.)

This book is here to change the way you think, the way you see your faith, and the way you live it out.

I pray you're blessed, encouraged, and even amused a little while reading it.

Because one thing is for sure: You were never meant to live powerlessly.

Now let's get started.

Chapter 1

# YEAH...THAT NEEDS TO BE CORRECTED

There was nothing better than a Friday night at the movies, especially when Blake and his friends were broke teenagers with just enough cash for a ticket and a questionable amount of buttery popcorn.

So there they were—Blake, Jordan, and Elijah—sitting in a packed theater, waiting for the movie to start. They hadn't actually agreed on what they were watching; Jordan had just randomly picked something that sounded "deep and artsy," and everyone else went along with it.

The theater was buzzing with the usual pre-movie chaos: people crunching on overpriced nachos, that one guy who was already coughing as though he needed medical attention, and the unmistakable sound of someone sneaking in snacks they definitely hadn't bought at the concession stand out front.

"Alright, guys, predictions?" Elijah leaned over, whispering as he shoveled a handful of popcorn into his mouth.

"I think it's gonna be one of those movies where everyone dies, and at the end we find out they were dead the whole time," Jordan said, stretching like some self-proclaimed movie analyst.

"Nah," Blake said, shaking his head. "It's gonna have some *huge* twist at the end that makes no sense, and people are gonna pretend they understand it so they don't feel dumb."

Elijah snorted. "You mean like every 'artsy' movie ever?"

Before they could continue roasting the film we hadn't even seen yet, the theater dimmed and the movie began.

And it was *weird*.

For the next two hours they sat there completely mesmerized but also deeply confused.

The film had talking animals that seemed as if they had *way* too much wisdom, a guy wandering through a desert *for no reason*, and at one point some kind of floating golden book that nobody read.

By the end the main character either died or became immortal—the guys weren't sure.

Then cut to black. Roll credits.

Dead silence.

Nobody in the theater moved. It was the kind of ending where people weren't sure whether they should clap, cry, or demand their money back.

Then Jordan just said exactly what they were all thinking.

"Bro. What. Did. We. Just. Watch?"

As the guys walked out of the theater into the bright lobby, it became clear they had all watched three completely different movies.

"Alright," Jordan said, rubbing his hands together. "Everyone say what they thought it was about."

Blake went first. "OK, listen. The whole thing was about spiritual warfare. The golden book was clearly the Bible, the desert was temptation, and the main guy was trying to find his purpose in God."

Jordan blinked. "No. No, that's not what happened."

Blake frowned. "Then what did you get out of it, *Mr. Film Expert*?"

Jordan crossed his arms, looking proud of himself. "It was obviously about the downfall of human ambition. The guy in the desert? That's corporate greed. The floating book? That was symbolic of knowledge lost in the digital age."

Blake stared at him for a long moment. "Are you OK?"

Elijah, who had been suspiciously quiet, suddenly burst out laughing.

Both Blake and Jordan turned to him. "What's so funny?"

Elijah wiped tears from his eyes. "You guys are so deep. You wanna know what I saw? That was 100 percent a superhero origin story. The main guy got powers from the golden book, but he rejected them because he was too emo. *Classic hero's journey.*"

Jordan gasped. "You're telling me you thought this was a superhero movie?"

Elijah shrugged. "I mean, he literally started glowing at the end. What do you call that?"

Jordan clutched his head. "We all watched three completely different movies."

At that moment Blake realized this was exactly how people approach faith.

He pointed at Jordan. "You're the overthinker. You take everything so intellectually that you miss the main message."

Jordan scoffed. "Wow. Rude."

Blake then pointed at Elijah. "You, my friend, are like those Christians who turn everything into Marvel."

Elijah grinned. "I *do* love a good origin story."

"And me?" Blake grinned. "I clearly saw the truth."

Jordan rolled his eyes. "Oh, so *you* were the only one who got the 'real' meaning?"

Blake shrugged. "Look, even Jesus had to explain His parables because people didn't get them."

Elijah nodded. "Yeah, but let's be real. Even if Jesus sat next to us during that movie, He'd probably be like, 'Yeah, I have no idea what that was about either.'"

Just as the guys were about to leave, they noticed an old man standing by the concession stand, staring at them.

He looked mystical—like the kind of guy who would either say something life-changing or try to sell them essential oils.

"You boys liked the movie?" he asked, his voice strangely deep.

Jordan answered first. "We're, uh, still figuring that out."

The old man smiled. "Funny thing about stories," he said, tapping the counter. "People always see what they're ready to see."

They stared at him, half waiting for him to pull out a scroll and start reciting ancient wisdom.

He continued, "The truth isn't always complicated. But sometimes people make it that way."

Then he grabbed his popcorn and walked out.

The boys all just stood there in stunned silence.

"Did we just get schooled by a random dude at the movie theater?" Elijah finally whispered.

Jordan shook his head. "I don't even know what's real anymore."

But deep down Blake knew what the old man meant.

We do that with faith all the time: Some of us overcomplicate it, some of us turn it into a feel-good superhero story, and some of us just don't get it at all.

But the truth is always there.

Clear. Simple. Unchanging.

Even in a movie no one understands.

## BUT...WE SAT THROUGH THE SAME SERMONS

One of the most impactful poems I've ever read is called "Our Deepest Fear." The poet shows us that our deepest fear is not that we are inadequate but that we are powerful beyond measure. What a profound statement!

But I'd like to challenge it slightly—not in its entirety but in one key area.

What if we replaced the word *inadequate* with *ignorant*? That shifts everything.

Now the question isn't "What if I'm too powerful?" but rather "How powerful am I, and why am I unaware of it?" This leads to an even deeper question: "Where does this power come from, and why are so many of us ignorant of it?"

Years ago a fellow parishioner from my church unexpectedly stopped by our home for a visit. I've always loved talking about Jesus—He's my favorite subject. Because of that I naturally assumed this woman would enjoy the conversation as much as I did. And at first she did.

But then something changed.

As our conversation continued, I began explaining how children of God don't fully understand the power they possess simply because of who their Father is. Our inheritance is filled with benefits, favor, and spiritual authority, yet so many of us walk around completely unaware of it. I even referenced the verse "Blessed be the Lord, who daily loadeth us with benefits" (Ps. 68:19, KJV).

That was when I noticed her expression shift.

She grew quiet. Her posture stiffened slightly. She looked almost uncomfortable.

I couldn't understand why.

Confusion settled in. After all, this woman and I listened to the same sermons. The pastor of our church spoke along the same lines as what I was saying. Had she been hearing differently?

I wasn't talking about something strange or new; I was sharing what the Bible already says. I wasn't claiming we had power outside God. I wasn't suggesting anything radical. I was simply stating a truth that, if fully understood, would change how we live as believers.

But for some reason this truth seemed unsettling to her.

That moment stayed with me.

Why do so many believers struggle with the idea that God has given us power? Why is it so hard to accept that as His children, we inherit privileges, authority, and divine benefits?

I believe the answer lies in ignorance.

If every last person alive today understood the significance of simply having been born, the world would look completely different.

Because whether people realize it or not, life itself is proof of value.

If you are breathing, you were created with purpose. If you are alive, you matter. If God saw fit to put you on this earth, you are worth something beyond measure.

But here's the problem: The enemy wants to keep people from knowing this.

Consider even having a name. At first glance having a name might not seem like a big deal. It might feel like an obvious, insignificant fact—everyone has a name, right?

But this goes deeper than you think.

Way deeper.

## THERE'S A BOOK OF...WHAT?

I'll never forget a beautiful autumn afternoon years ago when my children were still small. At first it felt like any other day: calm, routine, unremarkable. But as it turned out, it was anything but.

The late afternoon sunlight streamed through the windows, filling the house with a soft glow. Outside, the leaves rustled in the breeze, some drifting down and landing on the driveway. It was the usual sign that fall had fully settled in.

I heard the familiar sound of my husband, Ed, pulling into the garage. The hum of the garage door followed, and then the front door creaked open. I could hear his steps as he walked in, shaking off the chill of the air, with his jacket draped over one arm. Behind him came the sound of little feet moving quickly, full of excitement.

Our younger daughter burst through the door, just like she always did, filling the house with her energy.

"Hi, Mommy!" she called out, her voice bright and cheerful.

"Hi, baby!" I answered, smiling as she ran straight to me, with arms outstretched. I knelt down to catch her, and she threw herself into my arms. Her small frame pressed into mine, and I held her tight. These were the moments I never wanted to take for granted—the kind that felt small but meant everything.

She pulled back, her eyes wide with excitement, and dug into her school bag. After some searching, she pulled out a piece of construction paper, which was bent and slightly crumpled from being carried around all day. She held it up to me with both hands like it was the most important thing in the world.

"There's a Book of Life in heaven," she said with confidence.

I nodded. "You're right. The Bible tells us that."

I thought that was the end of it, but then she continued innocently, "—and there's a book of death in hell with people's names too."

I stopped.

For a second, I wasn't sure what to say. Where had she

## Yeah...That Needs to Be Corrected

heard that? Had they taught this at her Christian school? Was this some new teaching I wasn't aware of? My mind started racing. "What does she mean? Is this something she picked up somewhere?" My thoughts jumped in every direction.

But then, just as quickly, I heard something else.

A voice.

It wasn't my daughter's. It wasn't Ed's. And it wasn't my own.

It was the voice of the Lord.

Clear. Firm. Unshaken.

"No, there's not."

Three words. That was it.

But they settled deep in my spirit, stopping my thoughts in an instant. It wasn't a question or a debate; it was a correction.

I looked back at my daughter, who was still holding her paper and waiting for me to respond.

I smiled at her and said, "God says there's no book of death in hell, sweetheart."

She nodded, accepting it without hesitation. Just like that, she moved on to something else, as children do.

But I didn't move on.

That moment stayed with me. A seed had been planted in my heart, even if I didn't realize it yet. It was the moment that, later, would lead me to write this book, *The Devil's Greatest Fear.*

At first I kept wondering, "Why did her words hit me so deeply? Why did God step in so quickly to correct what was said?" Then it became clear.

The devil has spent centuries twisting the truth, spreading lies to keep people confused, afraid, and bound.

He wants to distort what God says because if people don't know the truth, they can't walk in it. My daughter, without realizing it, had repeated a lie that was told to her, and God wasted no time in setting it straight.

It made me wonder, "How many of the things we believe just because we've heard them so many times that aren't really true? How many ideas have we accepted that never came from God?"

The more I thought about it, I saw that my daughter may not have fully understood what she was saying, but God had used her to expose something important.

Children have a way of doing that, don't they? They speak with honesty. They don't filter things the way adults do. They don't overthink their words. They ask questions we wouldn't dare ask. They see the world in ways we've forgotten how to see.

And sometimes God speaks through them in ways that tend to stop us in our tracks.

That moment with my daughter wasn't just a passing conversation. It was a lesson, a reminder, and a warning.

As you go through this book, I hope you'll see why this moment mattered—not just to me but to all of us. It wasn't just about correcting a child's misunderstanding.

It was about something much deeper.

One must not forget: The devil has a perfect track record of thriving on deception. If he can twist one truth, he can shift an entire generation.

This is why we must be careful what we believe, what we accept, and what we repeat.

That moment taught me something I'll never forget:

Even in everyday conversations, God is speaking. Even

in the smallest moments, He is revealing truth. Even when we're not looking for it, He is guiding us.

The only question is "Are we paying attention?"

# Chapter 2

# WHO DO YOU THINK YOU ARE?

If you had asked Jonah three months ago who he was, he would've given you a simple answer: "I'm Jonah. Thirty-four. I work in sales. I like basketball. I hate seafood. I have a cat named Milo." End of discussion.

But if you asked him now? He wouldn't have an answer.

Because Jonah can't remember his name.

It wasn't amnesia—not in the dramatic, movie-style way where someone wakes up in a hospital with no memory of their past. No, this was something else. Something *worse*.

It started with a phone call.

"Hello?" Jonah answered groggily one night, rubbing his eyes.

The line crackled, and then a voice—calm, steady, and unfamiliar—spoke.

"You don't know who you are."

Jonah sat up. "Excuse me?"

"You don't know who you are," the voice repeated.

He frowned. "Listen, buddy, I don't have time for prank calls—"

Click.

The line went dead.

Weird.

But Jonah was a practical guy. He chalked it up to a wrong number, shrugged it off, and went back to bed.

Then strange things started happening.

At work his boss stopped mid-sentence while trying to call his name.

"Hey, uh...you. Can you send me that report?"

Jonah thought nothing of it. People forget names all the time, right?

Then his barista, who had been serving him the same coffee order for two years, hesitated before handing him his drink.

"Here you go, sir."

*Sir?*

And then things got worse.

He received an email at work—*addressed to him*—but instead of his name, the recipient line just said, "To: [Redacted]."

His driver's license? The ink on his name had smudged, making it unreadable.

His credit card? Declined. When he called the bank, the representative said, "I'm sorry, sir, but I can't seem to find your account."

That's when the panic set in.

Jonah rushed to the DMV, slammed his ID onto the counter, and demanded an explanation.

The clerk looked at the card and then at him. "Sir, you didn't put your name down."

## Who Do You Think You Are?

Jonah's pulse quickened. "What are you talking about? My name *is* there!"

The clerk flipped the card around. The name field was blank.

Jonah's throat went dry. He had *written* his name. He knew he had.

Hadn't he?

"Sir?" The clerk gave him a concerned look. "Do you need medical assistance?"

Jonah stumbled out of the DMV, heart hammering in his chest.

His name was gone.

Not forgotten.

Gone.

That night he stood in front of his bathroom mirror, gripping the sink. His reflection stared back at him, but something was...off. His jawline looked softer. His brown eyes were duller. The face was *his*, but at the same time it wasn't.

He grabbed his phone and scrolled through his contacts.

Mom. Dad. Friends.

But as he scrolled, something terrifying happened.

The names—one by one—vanished.

Flickering out like a glitching screen until his contact list was completely, terrifyingly blank.

His breath hitched.

Then his phone rang.

*Unknown Number.*

A chill crawled up his spine.

He hesitated and then answered.

"Hello?"

The same voice from before. Calm. Unbothered.

"You don't know who you are."

Jonah swallowed hard. "Who are *you*?"

The voice chuckled, slow and deliberate. "That's the wrong question."

Jonah gripped the phone. "Then what's the right one?"

A pause. Then—

"Who are you?"

Jonah opened his mouth, but nothing came out.

Because for the first time in his life he didn't know.

The voice continued. "People think their name is just a label. Just a word. But it's more than that. Your name tells you who you are. And when it's taken from you—"

Jonah's stomach clenched. "What happens?"

A pause. Then—

"You disappear."

A click. The call ended.

Jonah stared at the screen, his breath coming in short gasps.

A message popped up.

*Find out who you are. Or be forgotten forever.*

Jonah didn't sleep that night.

The next morning he tried to act normally. But the world didn't see him the same way.

People hesitated before speaking to him. Some

*Who Do You Think You Are?*

squinted like they were trying to remember who he was. Others ignored him completely, as if he were...fading.

As if he were becoming *nothing*.

Then, just when he thought all hope was lost, a stranger sat beside him on a park bench.

An old man. Wrinkled hands. Sharp eyes. A knowing smile.

"You're looking for something," the man said.

Jonah turned, heart pounding. "How do you know?"

The man chuckled. "I see things. And I know when someone's losing themselves."

Jonah hesitated and then whispered, "I don't remember my name."

The man nodded as if he had heard this before.

"Then it's time you find out who you *really* are."

Jonah swallowed. "And how do I do that?"

The man smiled. And for the first time in days Jonah felt something stir in his chest:

*Hope.*

Because maybe, just maybe, he wasn't lost forever.

Maybe he could *remember*.

## MORE THAN A LABEL

Roman-born Holocaust survivor Elie Wiesel once shared that when the Nazis captured him during World War II, they tattooed a number on his arm. At that moment they took away his name and identity.

Why did he say this, and what did he mean by it? It might be tempting to think, "It's just a tattoo. It's just a number." But that mindset misses the point entirely. It wasn't *just* anything. That number wasn't a mark of belonging or even survival; it was a calculated attempt to strip him of everything that made him human.

The untold truth is that a name is more than a label; it's a connection to who you are. It's tied to your story, your memories, and your purpose. Without it you're untethered like a ship adrift with no anchor. Names give us a place in the world.

So when Wiesel said that losing his name felt as if he had lost his identity, he wasn't exaggerating. The Nazis sought to erase the essence of who he was, and they did so in a way that robbed him of hope, dignity, and individuality.

This practice of stripping away names is not unique to the Holocaust. Since the beginning of time, slavery has been a part of human history, and it nearly always involves the erasure of identity. When a person is taken captive, often the first thing that happens is their name being changed. Slaveholders know that taking away a person's name is a way to dehumanize them and make them feel like nothing more than property. Across generations, those who were enslaved described feeling invisible—like they no longer existed as individuals. Without names, they were reduced to something that could be bought, sold, or discarded.

It's not just a historical issue, though. Even in modern prisons this pattern continues. Globally when someone is incarcerated, their name is replaced with a number. It's not just administrative; it's dehumanizing. Prisoners often describe feeling like they've been reduced to nothing more than statistics, or numbers in a system. It's no accident that many of them say things such as "I feel like I'm nobody."

Here's the bigger question: "Why does losing a name—losing identity—cut so deeply?"

It's because at our core we all long for significance. We're all searching for purpose. Our greatest fear isn't failure; it's being nobody, or not existing in any meaningful way. Even those who seem proud or self-assured wrestle with this question deep down: "Why am I here?"

You may never have asked yourself that question, but if you haven't, you probably are asking it now—or you will eventually—because none of us wants to simply go through the motions of life. We all want to know that we matter.

Here's the truth: You were made in God's image. That fact alone changes everything. It means you are the most valuable creation on earth. God made this clear in Genesis when He said, "Let Us make man in Our image, according to Our likeness" (v. 1:26). Nothing else in creation was given this distinction. Sure, the Bible says we're a little lower than the angels for now, but even angels don't bear the image of God. And God promises that one day, we will surpass them and be more like Him.

Let's step back and think about creation itself. God didn't just form the earth, plunk us on it, and then say, "Here, survive." No, He created the perfect environment for us to thrive in. Imagine you had a child, watched them grow up, saw them get married, and wanted to provide the new couple with the best possible home. Would you give them an empty plot of land and say, "Here, figure it out"? Or would you hand them a half-built house and say,

"At least you have a roof over your head"? Of course not. A loving parent wouldn't do that.

God didn't either. When He created the earth, He thought of every detail. He created the sun to provide warmth and light. He made the moon to regulate gravity and to guide us at night. He filled the earth with soil to grow food, water to sustain life, and trees to provide shelter and beauty. He even created flowers—not because we needed them but because He wanted us to have something beautiful to enjoy. Everything in creation was formed with us in mind.

All that God created in earth was made *for* us, not the other way around.

When God created Adam, He didn't stop there. He said, "It is not good that man should be alone" (Gen. 2:18). So He created Eve. And not just Eve—God also formed every animal, every bird, every living thing. He wanted Adam and Eve to have everything they needed to live abundantly and thrive. This is how much God loves us.

Everything in nature reflects God's care for us. I live near the Rocky Mountains, and every time I see them, I'm reminded of His greatness. Those mountains weren't an accident; God crafted them for us to enjoy. No matter how advanced humanity's technology becomes, nothing we create will ever match the perfection of His work. Human creations always have flaws because they're not formed by the perfect hands of the Creator.

Why does all this matter? Because if you understand how much God values you, you'll start to see yourself differently. You'll realize that your worth isn't tied to what others think or say. Your value is intrinsic, eternal, and unshakable.

*Who Do You Think You Are?*

Yet so many people spend their lives chasing fame or validation, thinking that being "somebody" will give them significance. They don't realize they *already are somebody*. If you're alive, breathing, and walking this earth, you have a purpose. You're more valuable than any other species on this planet. And this is one reason the devil despises you. He knows how much God treasures you, and he'll do everything in his power to keep you from discovering it.

From the moment you were born, the devil has been working against you. Often he starts with your family, using generational patterns to create footholds. Sororities, fraternities, Freemasonry, occult practices are just a few of the ways doors can be opened to spiritual attacks. Personal sins such as lying, jealousy, and sexual sin—including homosexuality, adultery, and fornication—can give him a foothold. This is why it's so important to examine our hearts daily. Ask God to reveal anything that might be standing in the way of your purpose.

Deliverance is real, and I've seen it change lives. I know ministers who've witnessed generational curses broken. When people are set free, it doesn't just affect them; it transforms their families. Health issues disappear, financial struggles lift, and peace floods their homes. God's power is limitless, and His love for you is boundless.

So let me ask you this: If I were to inquire who you are—beyond your name, career, or family role—could you confidently answer? Because if you know who you are in Christ, it doesn't matter if the world does. Knowing your identity is the first step toward walking into your God-given purpose. And once you embrace that, nothing can stop you.

# Chapter 3

# STOP CHASING TITLES AND START LIVING YOUR PURPOSE

If you've ever wanted to see two people who lived the same life but walked two completely different paths, let me tell you about Walter Bridges and Jim Callahan.

Walter and Jim had a lot in common. They were the same age, attended the same university, and were employed by the same prestigious company straight out of college. They were equally intelligent, equally hardworking, and equally ambitious. If you had met them when they were twenty-five, you would've thought they were both headed for greatness.

But by the time they hit fifty-five, they were standing in two entirely different worlds.

Walter was somebody—or at least that's how he saw himself. He had climbed the corporate ladder, grabbed every promotion, and made sure everyone within a ten-mile radius knew his full title: senior vice president of global strategy and business development for high-yield market growth initiatives and emerging technologies. (Yes, that was the *actual* title on his business card.)

Jim, on the other hand?

Jim was just...*Jim*.

While Walter was racking up promotions, Jim had quietly stepped away from the corporate grind after realizing he didn't like working eighty-hour weeks just to be able to afford a slightly shinier car. Instead, he started his own small business: a little bookshop downtown. It wasn't flashy, but it was his. And more importantly it made him happy.

But Walter? Walter never understood that.

He *needed* to be important. He *needed* people to see him as someone of significance. Titles were his currency, and respect was his addiction. He wasn't just Walter—he was Mr. Bridges, and if you forgot to call him that, he'd correct you faster than a GPS recalculating a wrong turn.

And then one fateful day everything changed.

Walter had spent years working toward a single goal—becoming CEO. And finally it was within reach.

The board of directors had called him in for a meeting. He straightened his tie, checked his Rolex, and strutted into that boardroom like a king walking to his coronation.

And then disaster struck.

The chairman leaned forward, cleared his throat, and said the words that shattered Walter's perfectly curated reality.

"We've decided to go in a different direction."

Walter blinked. "I—I'm sorry, what?"

"The board has decided that we need fresh leadership. Someone with a *modern* approach."

## Stop Chasing Titles and Start Living Your Purpose

Walter's jaw clenched. "Who?"

The chairman folded his hands. "Michael Carter."

Walter nearly fell out of his chair.

Michael Carter? The *intern* from ten years ago? The kid who used to spill coffee and get lost in the office hallways? *That* Michael Carter?

Walter tried to compose himself. "With all due respect, I have *three decades* of experience. I have overseen mergers, acquisitions, and billion-dollar deals! I've spent my entire career preparing for this position!"

The chairman nodded sympathetically. "Yes, Walter, and we respect your contributions. But the company needs fresh ideas."

Walter's face burned. His title and his prestige were gone in an instant.

And for the first time in his life he realized something terrifying.

Without his title...

He had no idea who he was.

On the same afternoon that Walter's world collapsed, Jim was standing in his little bookshop, whistling as he restocked a shelf.

A customer walked in—an old man with kind eyes who had been coming to Jim's shop for years.

"Jim," the man said, smiling, "I just wanted to say something. I come here every week, and it's always the best part of my day. This place reminds me of when I used to go to the library with my dad as a kid. You have no idea how much that means to me."

Jim grinned. "Well, I'm glad you keep coming back."

The man chuckled. "You know, people spend their lives trying to build something that lasts. And most of them think it has to be something *big*. But what you've built here? It lasts. It matters."

Jim paused, letting those words sink in.

It wasn't about money. It wasn't about power. It was about impact—about making a difference in people's lives, no matter how small.

Jim didn't have a fancy title. He didn't need one.

Because he already knew who he was.

It took Walter a long time to come to terms with his fall from corporate royalty. He went through the classic stages: denial, anger, bargaining, and rage-typing emails he never sent.

For months, he walked around like a man who had been exiled from his own kingdom. He thought about writing a tell-all book. He thought about starting his own consulting firm just so he could slap a new, impressive title on his LinkedIn profile.

But then, one evening, he found himself standing in front of a small bookshop.

Jim's bookshop.

Walter stepped inside, half out of curiosity, half out of desperation.

"Walter!" Jim called from behind the counter. "Long time no see!"

Walter hesitated. He hadn't seen Jim in over twenty years. And yet Jim greeted him like an old friend.

## Stop Chasing Titles and Start Living Your Purpose

Jim motioned for him to sit down. "So what's new?"

Walter sighed, rubbing his temples. "I...lost my job."

Jim nodded. "Yeah, I heard."

Walter looked at him, surprised. "You *heard*?"

Jim grinned. "Walter, you made the news. 'Corporate Titan Falls from Grace!' It was on three different websites."

Walter groaned, sinking into the chair. "Great."

Jim poured them both a cup of coffee. "So... what's next?"

Walter shook his head. "I have no idea. My whole life was about climbing that ladder. And now I don't even know where I'm standing."

Jim leaned back, studying him. "You know what your problem is, Walter?"

Walter exhaled. "Please, enlighten me."

Jim smirked. "You spent your whole life being *somebody* instead of *being yourself*."

Walter scoffed. "What does that even mean?"

Jim set his cup down. "You were so busy chasing titles that you forgot who you were without them. You thought success was about power, but real success? It's about purpose."

Walter looked around the shop. It wasn't impressive. It wasn't grand. But it was something real.

Something built on identity, not ego.

Walter sighed, shaking his head. "So what do I do now?"

Jim smiled. "Well, for starters, stop trying to be

27

Mr. Bridges, corporate giant, and start figuring out who Walter *actually* is."

Walter looked at Jim, then at the shelves of books, and then at his reflection in the window.

And for the first time in his life he realized...

He wasn't sure.

But maybe—just maybe—he was about to find out.

## That's *Doctor* to You!

Years ago when I worked for a successful small business, I learned a lesson I didn't realize would stick with me for so long. The business wasn't a corporate giant, but the owner ran it with pride and a personal touch that made it stand out from competitors.

On my first day he explained something that seemed unusual but quickly made sense. He said, "We're a first-name-basis company." He emphasized that no matter who the client was or how high their position, they were to be addressed by their first name. He believed this approach made the company feel approachable, welcoming, and even human.

The owner was proud of this policy, and I followed his instructions carefully. Every client I encountered, no matter their status or profession, was greeted by their first name. The interactions were always smooth, and clients appreciated the friendly atmosphere we created. Conversations were warm, and the work always got done.

That was the way it worked—until one day when I was

instructed to contact a particular client. She was a doctor, and we'll call her Kathy.

I remember that day vividly. I picked up the phone, called Kathy's number, and introduced myself in my usual tone. "Hi, may I speak with Kathy?"

Her response came fast and sharp, and it caught me completely off guard. "You mean *Dr.* Kathy," she snapped.

I paused, confused. "Dr. Kathy? But this isn't a medical call!" I thought. Still, I repeated my question, unsure of what to make of her tone. "May I speak with Kathy?"

Her voice cut through the air again, this time more insistent. "That's *Dr.* Kathy to you."

At that moment I froze. My thoughts were racing. Why was she so adamant about her title? Did she think I was trying to disrespect her? I wasn't being rude; I was just following the company's policy. I wasn't her patient, so this wasn't a medical consultation. After her repeated demands, I decided not to argue and moved forward with the purpose of the call. But I'll never forget that day—not because of what we discussed but because of what her insistence on being called "Dr." revealed.

It wasn't her title that stuck with me. It wasn't even that she corrected me. It was her *insistence*. I was dumbfounded by how deeply she tied her identity to her title, as if being addressed by her first name somehow diminished her value. It made me think about how often people cling to their titles, not realizing how much weight they place on something that isn't even who they are.

Here's the thing: I completely understand that people work hard to earn their titles. They dedicate years to education, training, and practice to reach the positions they're in, and they deserve to be recognized for their achievements. But issues arise when their need for recognition spills into their personal lives. When someone can't separate who they are from what they do, that's when their title becomes a crutch, a barrier, or even a source of pride.

## The Burden of Titles

Reflecting on that interaction, I realized how deeply some people will cling to titles as a source of identity. Titles, while often earned through hard work and dedication, can become a crutch. For many, titles are a way to prove their worth. They're a shield to hide behind and a way of saying, "Look at me. See how important I am."

But what happens when a title is stripped away? What happens when retirement, failure, or even circumstances beyond your control take away what you've relied on to feel valuable? What's left then?

History offers countless examples of people who tied their identities to their titles, only to lose everything when those titles no longer mattered. Consider King Nebuchadnezzar, the ruler of Babylon, who was consumed by his pride. In Daniel 4:30, he boasted, "Is not this great Babylon, that I have built for a royal dwelling by my mighty power and for the honor of my majesty?" But God humbled him in an instant. Nebuchadnezzar lost his kingdom and was reduced to living like an animal until he acknowledged God's sovereignty.

## When Titles Become a Crutch

Titles can become a crutch—something we lean on to feel important or valued. But here's the truth: Your title is not

## Stop Chasing Titles and Start Living Your Purpose

your identity. It's your role, your duty—it's what you *do*, not who you *are*.

Consider the great men and women of faith who changed the world for the kingdom of God: Billy Graham, Reinhard Bonnke, Kathryn Kuhlman, Smith Wigglesworth, and many others. None of them are remembered for their titles. They're remembered for their works. Their impact was tied not to a label but to the lives they touched and the gospel they spread. Their humility allowed God to use them mightily, and that's what made them great.

One of the most powerful examples of this is Mother Teresa. She wasn't concerned with titles or recognition. Her life was a testimony to humility and service. Her identity wasn't rooted in accolades or earthly praise; it was rooted in her purpose—to love and serve others as Christ did.

Did you know that the only people in the Bible who insisted on being addressed by their titles were the Pharisees and figures like King Nebuchadnezzar? If you search the Scriptures, you'll never find Jesus demanding that people address Him by His title, even though He was more deserving of it than anyone who ever walked the earth. On the rare occasions when people called Him by His titles, He humbly received it, but He never required it. He knew who He was.

Imagine the richest man in the world, Elon Musk (as of 2025), suddenly finding himself stranded on North Sentinel Island. This remote land, home to the Sentinelese people, is famously isolated from modern society. These tribespeople have never encountered the luxuries of the modern world: no smartphones, no internet, and certainly no electric cars or rockets. They live simply—speaking their own language, following their own ways, and rejecting all contact with the outside world. To them life is defined by what surrounds them, not by distant technologies or status symbols.

Now, picture Elon Musk stepping onto the island. Imagine him announcing, "Hey guys, I'm Elon Musk. I'm the richest man in the world! Get this: I make electric cars and rocket ships!"

How do you think they'd respond?

They wouldn't be impressed, let alone moved by his accomplishments or wealth. His title, which holds so much weight in the modern world, would carry no significance in their eyes. To them he'd be just another outsider.

This sharp contrast shows just how meaningless titles can be in the wrong context, in the wrong hands, or when presented to people who value their identity over status.

The truth of the matter is this: Titles are fleeting, but when God calls you by name, it holds eternal significance. Walking confidently in your God-given identity transforms everything, especially how you see yourself and how you understand your worth. And here's a truth that many people overlook: The devil has no name, which is why he desperately wants you to lose yours.

## When Titles Become Manipulative

Insisting on titles can also become a way to manipulate how others see us. When someone demands to be addressed by their title, they're often saying, "See me the way I want to be seen, not as I truly am." But God doesn't look at titles. He looks at the heart.

Even angels in the Bible didn't insist on their titles. When the archangel Gabriel appeared to Mary, he didn't introduce himself as "archangel Gabriel." He simply said, "I am Gabriel, who stands in the presence of God, and was sent to speak to you and bring you these glad tidings" (Luke 1:19). Similarly, when Michael is mentioned in Scripture, he's identified by his name, not by his title. These mighty beings didn't need to cling to titles because their authority came from God.

## THE MAN WHO "NEEDED" RECOGNITION

Years after my interaction with Kathy, I encountered another example of title-driven pride. I was assigned to do continual work for a man in Connecticut who had a reputation for being accomplished and well-connected. When I arrived at his office, he greeted me warmly but quickly began listing his accolades. He talked about the people he knew, the TV shows he'd been on, and the prestigious roles he'd held.

At one point he leaned back in his chair, folded his hands over his stomach, and said, "I don't think you realize who I am. I've been on the *Today Show, Good Morning America,* and other major programs."

I nodded politely, but inside I was trying not to laugh. "You're not Jesus. Why does it matter?" I thought. Of course, I didn't say that out loud, but his need for validation was palpable. He wanted so badly to be "somebody," not realizing he already was.

This encounter stayed with me because it illustrated how desperately people chase recognition. But as Solomon wrote in Ecclesiastes 1:14, "I have seen all the works that are done under the sun; and indeed, all is vanity and grasping for the wind." Titles and earthly accolades are fleeting, but the purpose God gives us is eternal.

## AHHH...*GLADIATOR*

*Gladiator* is, in my opinion, one of the hands-down best movies of all time. When this movie came out, I had no idea what to expect. The only thing I remember before its release is that the news kept emphasizing how gory it was and that there hadn't been many movies, if any, like it at the time.

I don't remember how I ended up going to see this film, but when I did, I felt like it somehow helped me look at life a little bit differently. I know the plot may seem like an oxymoron—a Roman general becoming a slave and a gladiator—but for me it went far deeper than that.

Most of us know the story of what happened to the main character of this film: A high-ranking general in the Roman army, Maximus, is corruptly stripped of his title, rank, and duties, and on top of that, his family is murdered. He is then forced into slavery, where he fights as a gladiator for Roman entertainment.

But the part that has stuck with me for well over twenty years now is Maximus's response when his rival, the evil and heartless Emperor Commodus, asks who he is. He responds with authority, "My name is Maximus Decimus Meridius, commander of the armies of the north, general of the Felix Legions, and loyal servant to the *true* emperor, Marcus Aurelius. Father to a murdered son, husband to a murdered wife." It was the mic drop heard in every theater around the world! It was the moment when the whole audience went, "Whew!" with downright gratification.

Throughout the film Maximus couldn't care less about his name or title. The other gladiators even called him "Spartan" at first, yet he never corrected them. It wasn't until Commodus, who murdered his own father to steal his royal position, forced him that he confessed who he was.

Maximus never forgot who he was or what his duty and command were. After he stated his real name and title, he went into his duties and personal identity. He never forgot what he was called to do, and he was loyal to it. He never corrected anyone when they called him Spartan, and he never seemed playful when they learned his name and began to chant it throughout the streets and the Colosseum. His main focus was always the task at hand and what he was put on this earth to do.

This is what every one of us needs to grasp firmly. We need to know who we are and what we are here to do. No one is here by mistake or by accident, and everyone is here to contribute in some way. God is a God of order and perfection. He is a big God with a big vision, and He uses us to fulfill that mission.

So the questions now are these: "Who are you?" "Why are you here?" "What is the task at hand?" and last but not least, "Are you fulfilling that purpose right now?"

## Biblical Perspective on Purpose over Titles

The Bible is filled with examples of people whose purpose was greater than their title. Take David, for instance. Before he became king, David was a shepherd—a lowly, overlooked person. But God chose him not because of his status but because of his heart. In 1 Samuel 16:7, God instructs the prophet Samuel concerning one of Jesse's other sons, "Do not look at his appearance or at his physical stature, because I have refused him. For the Lord does not see as man sees; for man looks at the outward appearance, but the Lord looks at the heart."

Another example is Mary, the mother of Jesus. She wasn't a queen or a woman of high status. She was a humble young woman from a small town. Yet God chose her for one of the most significant roles in history: bringing the Savior into the world. Her response to the archangel Gabriel in Luke 1:38 shows her humility: "Behold the maidservant of the Lord! Let it be to me according to your word."

God has given each of us incredible gifts: the ability to be humble, to love, and to cultivate a servant's heart. But the devil counterfeits these gifts by offering pride, selfishness, and a hunger for recognition. He tempts us to chase after titles and accolades. He enjoys distracting us from our true purpose. He whispers lies such as "If you achieve this, people will finally respect you" or "If you earn that title, you'll matter."

For example, someone might pursue a title such as "pastor" or "apostle" not because they feel called to serve but because they crave the recognition that comes with it. This is why Jesus warned in Matthew 6:1, "Take heed that you do not do your charitable deeds before men, to be seen by them. Otherwise you have no reward from your Father in heaven."

But these are empty promises. Your value isn't tied to what you achieve. It's tied to what Christ has already done for you.

## PRACTICAL STEPS TO BREAK FREE

So how do we break free from the trap of chasing titles? Here are five steps:

1. **Seek God *first*!** Matthew 6:33 reminds us to "seek first the kingdom of God and His righteousness, and all these things shall be *added* to you" (emphasis added).

2. **Examine your heart.** Psalm 139:23 says, "Search me, God, and know my heart; try me, and know my anxieties." Regularly ask God to reveal any pride or insecurity that may be lurking there.

3. **Serve humbly.** Jesus said in Mark 10:45, "The Son of Man did not come to be served, but to serve."

4. **Focus on eternal rewards.** Colossians 3:23–24 says, "And whatever you do, do it heartily, as to the Lord and not to men, knowing that from the Lord you will receive the reward of the inheritance; for you serve the Lord Christ."

5. **Remember your identity in Christ.** Ephesians 2:10 says, "For we are His workmanship, created in Christ Jesus for good works, which God prepared beforehand that we should walk in them."

When we stand before God, He won't ask about the letters before or after our names. He'll ask about the lives we touched and the love we showed. Titles fade, but purpose endures. Stop chasing titles. Start living your purpose.

# Chapter 4

# THE DEVIL HAS NO NAME

The ocean stretched endlessly before them, rolling in smooth, lazy waves that shimmered under the golden Hawaiian sun. The air smelled like salt and something sweet—maybe mangoes. Or maybe it was just the idea of mangoes.

Darren exhaled deeply, arms folded behind his head as he lay back on his beach towel. "You feel that, Jake?" he asked, cracking one eye open. "That's the feeling of not having to do anything. I think it's called happiness."

Jake, sitting stiffly in the sand next to him, was not relaxed. He glanced over his shoulder for what had to be the tenth time in five minutes. "Something's off about this place, man."

Darren groaned. "It's a resort, Jake. We are in literal paradise."

"I know. That's the problem."

Darren sat up, brushing sand off his arm. "Wow. You sound like those wacko guys on YouTube who think birds aren't real. What could possibly be 'off' about this place?"

Jake hesitated. "I don't know. It's just—" He rubbed the back of his neck. "Have you noticed no one's asked for our names since we got here?"

Darren frowned. "What?"

"The staff. The people we talk to. The surf instructor just called himself the guide. The guy at the front desk? The concierge. Even the lady at the tour desk? Your island host. What is that? A job title? A cult thing?"

Darren snorted. "You're seriously freaking out because people are on a first-name basis with themselves?"

"That's the thing." Jake turned to him, eyes dark. "They're not on a first-name basis. They're on a no-name basis."

Darren opened his mouth to shoot back some sarcastic remark, but...

Jake wasn't wrong.

Not once in the last three days had anyone introduced themselves with a name.

And now that he thought about it—no one had asked for theirs either.

A cold, sinking feeling crawled into Darren's stomach. "OK. That *is* weird."

Jake nodded. "And it gets weirder."

He dug into his backpack, pulled out a folded brochure, and slapped it onto Darren's lap. "Look at this," he said, tapping a section with his finger.

It was the resort's official pamphlet: a map of the property, a list of activities, and a few photos of smiling tourists in floral shirts pretending to have the time of their lives.

But when Darren's eyes scanned over the staff directory, his breath caught. There were no names.

*The Devil Has No Name*

Each employee was listed only by their title: The chef. The concierge. The housekeeper. The guide. The host.

Darren swallowed. "OK. Maybe it's like a theme. Some kind of gimmick. You know, 'mystery and exclusivity,' that kinda thing."

Jake shook his head. "Then why is it the guests too?"

Darren blinked.

Jake's voice dropped to a whisper. "Have you heard anyone introduce themselves?"

Darren thought back to the couple they'd met by the pool, the group they'd joined for zip-lining, and the friendly family they'd sat next to at dinner last night. They talked, laughed, and even shared stories. But not a single one had said their name.

Darren rubbed his temple. "OK. Now you're creeping me out."

"Good." Jake's leg bounced anxiously. "Because I think we need to leave."

Darren let out a sharp laugh. "Leave? Are you hearing yourself? We spent months saving for this trip! And you want to bail just because people here don't use name tags?"

Jake looked him dead in the eyes. "Last night. On the beach. That guy."

Darren's stomach dropped. *Oh. Right.*

Last night. The memory felt heavier now.

They had been walking along the shoreline, the waves cold against their ankles, when they saw him: a man standing at the water's edge, unmoving, staring out at the horizon.

At first he seemed normal...until they got closer. Until Darren realized he wasn't blinking.

The man turned his head just slightly—just enough for the moonlight to catch his face. That's when Darren saw it. Or rather, he didn't. The man's face had no...definition. Not like a blank slate—more like something unfinished—like a sculpture that had been abandoned before the details were carved in.

His lips moved. "You are travelers," the man said. His voice was smooth, even pleasant.

Darren forced a chuckle. "Yeah. Visiting for a couple of weeks."

The man's head tilted slightly. "You are passing through."

Not a question.

Jake had grabbed Darren's arm then. "Let's go."

As they turned to leave, the man smiled. It was the wrong kind of smile.

"You have names," he said. The way he said it—as if it were some rare, exotic thing—implied he didn't.

And then Darren had sworn he heard him whisper something under his breath. But it wasn't a word. It was a sound, as if someone were trying to remember how to speak.

They had practically sprinted back to their room after that, slamming the door, locking it, and pretending they weren't both completely freaked out.

And now, sitting here in the daylight, it all felt even worse.

Jake exhaled sharply. "Darren. We need to leave."

Darren finally nodded. "Yeah. OK. Let's go book an early flight."

They gathered their belongings, threw everything into their suitcases, and rushed to the front desk.

The concierge was already waiting for them.

He smiled. "Checking out early, gentlemen?"

Darren swallowed. "Yeah. We, uh, need to go."

The concierge nodded once and then slid a piece of paper across the desk. "If you could just sign here."

Darren reached for the pen—then froze. The form was blank. There was no check-in date. No checkout date.

And no names.

Jake grabbed his wrist. "Darren. Don't sign that."

The concierge's smile didn't falter, but something in his eyes shifted. Darren's pulse pounded. He let the pen slip from his fingers.

The concierge exhaled, like a parent sighing at a stubborn child. "Ah," he murmured. "You're smarter than most."

Darren's breath hitched, as he looked at the paper. Because beneath the blank space where their names should have been, something moved—like ink waiting to spill into form.

Jake didn't wait. He grabbed Darren's arm. "Run."

They didn't check out. Didn't wait for their bags. Didn't say goodbye to the staff that never said their names. And as they fled through the lobby, Darren realized something: No one tried to stop them because no one cared whether they left. Because no one had ever expected them to leave at all.

And behind them, at the front desk, the concierge stood still, staring at them with a polite, unreadable expression.

And the paper on the desk? The names never appeared because they had refused to give them. And in that place, that meant everything.

## He's a Nobody

Have you ever realized that the devil never addresses himself by name anywhere in Scripture? Not once. The archangels Gabriel and Michael did. But how can you introduce yourself if you don't have a name to give?

Have you ever paused to wonder why Jesus puts His *name* on our foreheads in the Book of Revelation, but the devil, attempting to mimic, can provide those who take the mark of the beast only with a *number* instead, which is 666?

Remember back in chapter 1, I mentioned how my daughter came home and said there was a Book of Death in hell with people's names in it, and then God immediately told me, "No, there's not"? That reminds me of when I was in fourth grade, attending a good private Christian school in northeast Philadelphia. It was there that I was trained in how to make dream catchers.

The teacher taught us that they were good to hang above our beds because it supposedly kept demonic or evil spirits away. But as many of us know, that couldn't be further from the truth. It does the opposite. (I remember my father confessing to me the one mistake he felt he made as a parent was that he trusted the Christian school system to help lead us spiritually. He said he realized that kind of training begins in the home and *continues* in the home.)

Back to the story: It wasn't until the interaction with my daughter that God took me on an in-depth journey of the truth behind what truly lies in hell and heaven, as well as on earth. You know how people will ask whether you want to hear the good part or the bad part first? In my experience, most people first ask for the bad part so they can get it over with—so I'm gonna go ahead with the bad part. Let's dive into what is truly in hell.

We know that those who do not accept Jesus Christ or who reject Him do not get to enter heaven but must go to the alternate location for eternity, which is, in fact, hell. There is no in-between place. If there's a place between heaven and hell, it would definitely be earth. It is *here* where we make the decisions for the Lord and our lives, and there is no other place. All decisions regarding our actions are made on planet Earth.

One day, God made it clear to me: There are no names in hell. No one is called by name. In other words, everyone is nameless.

Then He began to go into detail, explaining that everyone who has a name has a purpose because God is a God of purpose. Everything that God gives has a particular purpose and function. But when a person enters hell, all of that ceases to exist.

In the Bible Jesus speaks about some people being children of the devil: "You are of your father, the devil, and the desires of your father you want to do. He was a murderer from the beginning, and does not stand in the truth, because there is no truth in him. When he speaks a lie, he speaks from his own resources, for he is a liar and the father of it" (John 8:44).

As I meditated on what the Lord was teaching me, He took me on a journey that let me know that we, as human beings, can choose our Father. This relates to lordship and is analogous to being an orphan. Often, when a child in foster care reaches the age of twelve or so, he can accept or reject being adopted by a particular family.

In my first book, *I Saw God Last Night: Whoever Said He's Dead Flat-Out Lied*, I shared a story about a conversation I had with my grandmother's friend. One day we spoke on the phone, and the entire conversation was filled with nothing but glorifying God together.

After my grandmother's passing, her friend and I spent a lot of time reminiscing about her. Her friend shared many words of wisdom with me. But during one of our calls she said something that completely caught me off guard. She told me, "Not everyone is a child of God."

I was dumbfounded. I had always heard—through songs, sermons, and just about everywhere else—that everyone is a child of God. It sounded good, but as I later discovered, it simply isn't true. Scripture makes it clear in John 1:12, Romans 8:15–17, and Galatians 3:26 that we are adopted into the family of Christ, and only then do we truly become sons and daughters of God.

As we read previously, those who do not receive Jesus Christ are considered children of the devil. I know that may sound harsh, but the Word of God doesn't sugarcoat the truth. Scripture presents reality as it is—straightforward and without compromise. The Bible's purpose is not simply to make us feel all gooey inside; rather, it exists to guide, protect, and equip us to live the best life possible.

*The Devil Has No Name*

The Word of God is alive, and its purpose isn't to control us but to lead us into truth, helping us walk in His will so that, ultimately, we may enter the kingdom of God when we leave this earth.

Now, those of us who received Jesus Christ as our Lord and Savior and have truly surrendered to Him will receive the name of God on our foreheads, which is mentioned in Revelation 22:4: "They shall see His face, and His name shall be on their foreheads." This describes the redeemed in the New Jerusalem: those who will live in God's presence and be marked as His forever. It's also mentioned in the following verse:

> He who overcomes, I will make him a pillar in the temple of My God, and he shall go out no more. I will write on him the name of My God and the name of the city of My God, the New Jerusalem, which comes down out of heaven from My God. And I will write on him My new name.
> —REVELATION 3:12

Anyone who has a name—or is even worthy of having one—has a purpose. If you're alive, then your name carries meaning, and there's a reason behind it. A name isn't just something you have for the sake of it; it holds weight. It signifies identity, calling, and recognition. Even in the natural world, names are necessary for acknowledgment.

But in hell? There are no names because there is no purpose there. Everything in hell is void of meaning. There's no productivity, no future, nothing to look forward to, just endless emptiness. It's no coincidence that prisons around the world strip individuals of their names, reducing them to mere numbers. Would you believe that concept originated in hell and seeped into the earth? It's a reflection of a deeper spiritual reality: Where there is no name, there is no purpose.

Through the years, the Lord kept giving me revelation after revelation about the importance of names, the identity we have as believers, and the fact that we're not walking in our authority and purpose.

One day I sensed Him leading me to sit down and turn on the television in my living room. So I sat down on my tan sectional sofa, leaned back with the remote control, and flipped through the channels until I found a Christian network, where a preacher was speaking. He said something that piqued my interest because I had never heard it before, yet it paired with what God was revealing to me. He said, "The devil doesn't have a name, and no one knows what it once was."

I will never forget that. How could you hear something like that and forget it when all your life you've heard that the devil's name is Satan or that when he was in heaven, it had been Lucifer? Thanks to the leadership of God and this pastor's sermon, I came to find out the truth.

## A Leap of Faith

A couple of years later, our family decided to move to Colorado. We took a leap of faith because our charming little colonial house in the heart of Connecticut wouldn't sell. It had been sitting on the market for months, and despite our efforts no buyers came through. But after much prayer we felt led to trust God, pack up, and go, believing that He would take care of the rest. So that's exactly what

*The Devil Has No Name*

we did. And let me tell you, it was the true definition of *living on a prayer,* as Bon Jovi would say!

We loaded up our red Subaru Legacy, strapped in our two daughters, and drove across the country with no guarantees and little idea of what awaited us. When we arrived in Colorado, we lived out of suitcases in a hotel for a week, waiting to see where God would plant us. And sure enough He provided! After looking at rental house after rental house, we found a beautiful home just outside Colorado Springs, which was surrounded by stunning mountain views and crisp, fresh air. Our daughters made new friends, and we found ourselves immersed in Bible studies and services that enriched our faith even more. Looking back, it was one of those moments when we could see God's hand guiding every step, even when we had no idea what the next step would be.

One day I was invited to a women's group at a lovely Baptist church in a neighboring town. The woman who invited me was the mother of one of our youngest daughter's friends. She was beautiful and extremely intelligent. On top of that she was a seminary graduate. We sat together at a table with another group of women, and we all began to discuss Jesus and what He does in our lives, what He does and doesn't allow, and who we are in Him. Somehow we reached the topic of the devil.

I began to tell the other women how the Lord revealed to me that the devil has no name. It's neither Satan nor Lucifer. Everyone at the table became quiet, as you can imagine, because that's what the majority of the world has been taught to believe for so long. Then, all of a sudden, my friend broke the ice and said, "It's very interesting you say that because, when I was in seminary, they taught us that the term *satan* itself wasn't used in the Bible until a certain time frame. Before then the original reference to him was always *the satan*, and then they removed the word *the* to make it easier to read."

Wow! Can you say, "Revelation"? Making Scripture easier to read just gives the devil an identity that he doesn't even have! Whoever came up with this possibly had no idea (or maybe they did) that in removing the word *the* from *the satan*, they gave the devil a false identity.

We know all names begin with a capital letter. Before the change in grammar, satan was always lowercase. I hope you are still tracking with me; this is all about the subtle seeds of deceit.

## Where Did the Term *Lucifer* Come From?

Let's start with the term *Lucifer*, which is often misunderstood to be a name. Yet it is more of a title or job description, which means "light bringer" or "morning star."

Let's quickly touch on the origins of language. The word *Lucifer* is Latin. Early Christian Latin texts referred to the planet Venus, which is visible just before dawn and therefore associated with bringing light. In the biblical context, Lucifer is mentioned in Isaiah 14:12; the New King James Version describes the fall of a figure called "Lucifer, son of the morning." The passage most likely referred to a Babylonian king who was brought low despite his high status. Interpretations associated with the rebellious angel who fell from grace eventually linked the term with "Satan."

Isaiah 14 talks about a proud and arrogant king of

# The Devil Has No Name

Babylon who thought he was greater than he really was. This king believed that he was truly invincible; he even saw himself as comparable to God. He acted as though he could rise above the stars and take a place that was equivalent to God Himself. But because of his pride God sent a special message through the prophet Isaiah to let this king know that his time was up. This king's arrogance led to his downfall, and his empire collapsed. This was God's way of saying, "You may think you're on top, but you are just a man; you are just a human. I made you, and I will humble you."

Isaiah 14:12 uses some poetic and symbolic language that describes this fall, saying, "How you are fallen from heaven, O Lucifer, son of the morning! How you are cut down to the ground, you who weakened the nations!"

Here's where things get a little tricky. The word *Lucifer* in this verse doesn't mean what many people think it does. In the original Hebrew the word used is *hêlēl*. This translates to, as we discussed previously, "shining one" or "morning star" to describe the planet Venus because it's truly one of the brightest objects in the sky and appears before sunrise.[1] Therefore, when the verse says, "O Lucifer, son of the morning," the author is using poetic imagery to compare the pride of the king of Babylon to this bright star that seemed as if it would shine forever but eventually faded away. This illustrates that, just as the morning star disappears when the day begins, the king's glory and power will eventually vanish.

When the Bible was translated into Latin by a man named Jerome in the fourth century, the Hebrew word *hêlēl* was translated as "Lucifer," which means "light-bearer" or "morning star."[2] At the time Lucifer was not a name for the devil. It was just a descriptive word for something bright like Venus. But over time people started thinking that Lucifer was the proper name of satan or the devil. They assumed that Isaiah 14 was talking about the devil falling from heaven, but that's not what the chapter is talking about at all. So, if you were to read the whole thing, you'd see that it's all specifically directed at the king of Babylon, not a fallen angel or any kind of supernatural being.

So, why do people think this verse is about the devil? Probably because it's a lot like other Bible stories about the devil. For example, in Ezekiel 28, there is a prophecy about the king of Tyre that uses similar language. That passage describes a ruler who was proud and fell from a high position, and it also uses poetic imagery, comparing him to a perfect being in the Garden of Eden who is cast down because of his pride. Additionally, in Luke 10:18 Jesus specifically says, "I saw Satan fall like lightning from heaven." Then in Revelation 12, there's a drastic description of the devil being thrown out of heaven during a war with the angels. Because these stories all involve pride and being cast down, people start to connect them with Isaiah 14. So the idea that Lucifer was the devil's name became popular, even though the Bible never says that.

This misunderstanding became even more widespread after a man named John Milton wrote a famous poem called "Paradise Lost" in the 1600s. This is a fictional story about the devil's rebellion against God, and Milton uses Lucifer as the name of the devil. Milton's work was incredibly influential, and many people began to think this fictional portrayal of the devil was based entirely on the Bible. But as we discussed, according to the original

*The Devil Has No Name*

text in Isaiah, Lucifer is not a name at all; it's a way of describing the king of Babylon's arrogance and fall.

This matters because it teaches us to be careful when reading and interpreting the Bible. It is important for us to read the Bible ourselves and ask the Holy Spirit to interpret it. There's nothing better than getting the truth from the author rather than speculating about what it means. Isaiah 14 is not about the devil; it's about a human being who thought he was greater than he was. The word *Lucifer* was simply a poetic term for something bright like the morning star, but this has been misunderstood over the centuries. By studying the Bible in its original context, we can avoid these kinds of misunderstandings and see the true and deeper meaning behind the text.

So God's message in Isaiah 14 is pretty clear: Anyone who exalts themselves and tries to take God's place will be brought low. It's a warning about pride, not a story about the devil. This is why it's so vital to read the Bible carefully and understand where traditions and ideas come from—because not everything we hear about the Bible from other sources is true.

## WHERE DID THE TERM *SATAN* COME FROM?

Likewise, the word *satan* wasn't originally a name at all, and the Bible itself makes it clear that it was never meant to be one. Originally in the Hebrew scriptures, the term was *ha-satan*, which means "the accuser" or "the adversary." The *ha* literally means "the," marking it as a title, not a name. It described a role such as calling someone "the prosecutor" or "the enemy." It wasn't personal, it wasn't powerful, and it certainly wasn't the devil as we often think of him today.

In the Book of Job, *the satan* shows up in God's court (Job 1:6–12). He's not there as some rebel waging war against God; he's there to accuse Job, challenging his righteousness. He claims that Job is faithful only because God has blessed him, and he asks permission to test Job's faith. Notice this: *The satan* can't do anything without God's permission. He's not a rogue, independent being with power; he's under God's authority and can operate only within the limits God sets. The same thing happens in Zechariah 3:1–2, where *the satan* accuses Joshua, the high priest. Again, he's just doing what his title suggests—accusing.

At this point in Scripture *ha-satan* is a job title, not a personal identity. It simply describes someone who opposes or challenges, and it could be applied to anyone in that role. There's no individuality to this figure, no honor, and certainly no power of his own. This is important because people often elevate the devil to a position of strength that he never had.

The real shift from *ha-satan* to Satan happened much later, during the time leading up to the New Testament. By the time the Gospels were written, the term had dropped the article *the* and was used more like a name. In the New Testament the satan is portrayed as an enemy of God's work—tempting Jesus in the wilderness (Matt. 4:1–11), sowing evil, and opposing the church. But let's be clear: Even in these moments, he's still not an equal to God. He's a defeated enemy from the start—a created being whose rebellion sealed his eternal destruction. Any power he has is temporary and exists only because God allows it for His purposes.

## The Devil Has No Name

The devil is not even worthy of a name. Names in the Bible carry deep meaning, often reflecting someone's purpose or identity in God's plan. The devil doesn't deserve that kind of recognition. He's defined not by who he is but by what he does: oppose, accuse, and destroy. He's called satan because that's all he amounts to—an adversary. Nothing more.

This shift in how people viewed the word *satan*—from a role to a so-called name—was influenced by human tradition and interpretation. The Bible never gives the devil a name and for good reason. Giving him a name would give him significance, and he has none. He's a liar, a deceiver, and a thief whose destiny is already sealed in the lake of fire (Rev. 20:10). He has no true identity, no rightful place, and no power compared with God. He thrives on deception, tricking people into thinking he's more important than he is.

The truth is that satan is nothing but a defeated foe. His entire purpose is to oppose God and His people, but even then, he's on a leash. He operates only as much as God permits, and his end is already written. The Bible doesn't give him the dignity of a true name because he doesn't deserve it. Let's not elevate him in our minds or words. He's a fallen, powerless creature who's already lost. That's the truth, plain and simple.

Here's what you must understand—and when you do, your entire perspective should change: You have what the devil once had but can never have again—an identity, a name. With both comes purpose. When he was kicked out of heaven, everything from God was taken away from him. Therefore, if you or I give the devil a name, he'll gladly take it. According to Scripture, only God and human beings have the authority to give names. (See Genesis 2:19.) In the Bible God gives names to humans and those in the spiritual realm (such as angels). The first man, Adam, was told to name every living creature. The devil hates you because you are everything that he is not and never will be.

As long as you are walking on this green earth, no matter who you are or what you've done, your future can always be bright. Because you are alive and have a name—an identity—you can bring that name into eternity; you have a purpose. Everyone in heaven has a name, but no one in hell does. This is why the Bible says not to fear man who can kill the body but to fear God who can destroy the body and soul in hell (Matt. 10:28). We'll touch more on this later.

Therefore, let's sum up this chapter: The one who is vehemently set on attacking us without mercy is a literal *nobody*! He's the biggest loser with no identity. You have so much more power over him than you think—and by the time you finish reading this book, you'll understand why and how to use it against him.

# Chapter 5

# THE DEVIL CAN'T GIVE NAMES

Las Vegas was full of scams, but Frank Delano had perfected a con that even the slickest hustlers in town had to respect. He wasn't a pickpocket or a card shark. He didn't run a rigged roulette table or scam tourists out of their life savings at back-alley poker games. No, Frank's operation was *much* simpler.

He ran Delano's Pawn & Gold, a shop where people came to trade their most valuable possessions for quick cash. But unlike other pawnshops Frank paid top dollar for everything.

Gold? He'd give you double the market price. Diamonds? He'd pay as if it were straight from the queen's collection. Antiques? He didn't even haggle, just nodded, pulled out a fat stack of cash, and sent his customers on their way, feeling like they had struck gold.

And they *had*.

At least that's what they thought.

Until they tried to spend the money.

Frank's genius was in the execution.

Every dollar he handed out was fake.

Not the kind of counterfeit that fools banks or serious collectors—no, this was cheap, barely-passable-for-Monopoly-money fake. The trick was in *how* he used it.

He never let anyone count it in the shop. He moved fast, distracted them, and talked up the value of their items while shoving the cash into envelopes or bags.

By the time they realized the money was worthless, the pawned valuables had been melted down or resold to buyers for real cash—meaning there was no proof that the initial transaction ever happened.

And he got away with that for years.

Until one day he met the wrong customer.

It was a Thursday night, just after closing. Frank had counted his earnings and was locking up when the old man walked in.

Thin. Tall. Wearing a gray suit that looked a little too nice for this part of town.

"Sorry, pal," Frank said, flipping the sign on the front door to CLOSED. "We're done for the night."

The man smiled. "Oh, I think you'll want to make an exception."

Frank sighed. "Listen, I don't do late deals."

The man placed a black velvet pouch on the counter.

## The Devil Can't Give Names

Frank stopped talking.

It was heavy. The kind of weight that only real gold carries.

Curious, Frank loosened the strings and dumped the contents onto the counter.

Gold coins.

And not just any gold coins. These were old with markings he didn't recognize. They weren't chipped, weren't scratched, and weren't even worn.

They looked untouched—like they had been sitting in some hidden vault for centuries.

Frank picked one up, rolling it between his fingers. "Where'd you get these?"

The man shrugged. "They've been around."

Frank studied him. This guy was different. Something about him felt *off*—but gold was gold.

"What do you want for them?"

The man smiled. "What do you think they're worth?"

Frank grinned. That was his favorite question. He always made people think they were about to get a great deal when he was the one walking away richer.

He pulled out his special cash drawer—the one full of *the finest counterfeit bills money could buy*—and counted out a ridiculous amount.

"Here," Frank said smoothly, sliding the pile toward the man. "More than fair."

The man didn't reach for it.

Instead he tilted his head.

"You've been paying people with fake money for years, haven't you, Frank?"

Frank's grin froze.

His hands twitched. "I—what?"

The man chuckled. "Relax. I don't work for the feds."

Frank let out a breath he didn't realize he was holding.

But something still wasn't right.

"You gonna take the money or not?" Frank asked, shifting uncomfortably.

The man leaned in, his voice lowering.

"How does it feel, Frank?"

Frank frowned. "How does *what* feel?"

The man smiled again—except this time, it wasn't friendly.

"To know you've built everything you have...on nothing."

The words hit harder than Frank wanted to admit.

His palms felt sweaty. His head suddenly hurt.

"I don't know what you're talking about," he muttered.

The man chuckled, gathering up his gold coins. "You will."

And with that he turned and walked out the door.

That night everything changed.

Frank went home, but something felt different.

## The Devil Can't Give Names

His apartment—normally filled with things he had *earned* through his *brilliance*—suddenly felt empty.

The expensive watch on his wrist? Fake.

The leather wallet in his pocket? Fake.

The stacks of cash in his safe? All fake.

He knew that. He had always known that.

But for the first time it bothered him.

He had spent years fooling people. Stealing from them. Laughing about it.

But what did he have?

A pile of lies.

And no matter how much fake money he printed, he couldn't buy peace.

The next morning, Frank went to his shop.

He unlocked the door, stepped inside, and froze.

Everything was gone.

The counters? Empty.

The display cases? Smashed.

The safe? Wide open.

He ran to the back office, yanking open drawers and tearing through shelves.

Nothing.

No gold. No diamonds.

And worse—no real money.

It was as if someone had erased him overnight.

Frank stumbled back, chest heaving. His heart

pounded.

And then, from the corner of his eye, he spotted it:

A black velvet pouch sat on the counter.

The same one from last night.

With a shaking hand he opened it.

Inside there was one gold coin.

And etched into the surface, barely visible, was a single word:

"Nothing."

Frank dropped the coin as if it burned his hand.

His head was spinning. His knees felt weak.

Because he understood exactly what had happened.

For years, he had been paying people with nothing.

And now?

Nothing was all he had left.

Frank Delano thought he could cheat the system.

He thought he could build an empire on lies.

But the devil never pays his debts because deception only works...

Until it doesn't.

And in the end?

Frank wasn't just a con man.

He was his own best customer, buying into the biggest lie of all—that he could fool everyone, including himself.

## THE DEVIL CAN'T NAME—
## HE CAN ONLY LABEL

The devil has no power to give names. God holds that power and has generously given it to mankind and none other. Nowhere in Scripture do we see any being other than God and man bestowing formal names on anyone or anything.

We know that God named the angels—because how else would they have received their names? It is also God who named the universe and everything within it, including the first and second heavens. When we look at the beginning of creation, God personally named Adam in the Garden of Eden. But then something remarkable happened: God granted Adam the ability to name his wife, Eve.

This wasn't just a casual act; it was a divine privilege. Adam, representing mankind, was given the honor of naming every animal in the garden. From that moment on we see a pattern: Adam and Eve name their children, their children name theirs, and the pattern continues throughout human history. Naming is an act of God-given authority.

Since the enemy cannot create, he counterfeits. Unable to bestow real names, he resorts to name-calling, throwing out insults like "stupid," "loser," and "worthless." But these are not names at all; they are merely descriptors—labels meant to wound and deceive.

This deception runs deeper than we often realize. If we take it even further, we can consider this: Demons themselves do not have true names either—only functions.

Many wonder, "But don't demons give names when

called out during deliverance services?" It's a valid question. During spiritual warfare, deliverance ministers often ask demons for their names, and responses can vary widely. Some claim to be named Jezebel, Leviathan, or Beelzebub, but are these truly names or just descriptors or functions?

Here's the key to understanding this: Demons lie.

Jesus Himself stated that satan is the father of lies, and the truth is not in him (John 8:44). If every demon and unclean spirit is of the devil, then deception is ingrained in their nature. Their so-called names are nothing more than identifiers of their assignments. They do not carry the God-given authority that comes with a true name.

## THE POWER OF A NAME

God's act of naming is more than just assigning a title; it is an impartation of identity and purpose. That is why throughout Scripture, names hold deep significance. Abram became Abraham. Jacob became Israel. Simon became Peter. A name from God always signifies destiny, calling, and transformation.

The devil has no authority to do this. He cannot create identity. He can only try to destroy, distort, and deceive. But we are not defined by his labels—we are each defined by the name God has given us.

So the next time the enemy tries to whisper lies about who you are, remember this truth: The devil can throw labels at you, but your true name—your true identity—comes from God alone.

You might say, "But wait! In Mark 5:9, Jesus asked the demon-possessed man his name, and the demon responded! Doesn't that mean demons have names?"

## The Devil Can't Give Names

And you would be absolutely right in pointing that out. But let's take a closer look at what the demon said. The spirit's response was, "My name is Legion, for we are many."

Let's pause here for a moment. Legion is not a name; it's a description of quantity, power, and presence, but it's not an identity. And I truly believe Jesus allowed this conversation to be recorded in Scripture to indirectly show us that demons do not possess names, only functions.

Think about it: This is the only time in all of Scripture that Jesus ever asked a demon its "name." Just once. Every other time, He simply commanded them to leave—no introductions, no interrogations, no discussion—only authority. If knowing demons by name was important, don't you think Jesus would have asked every time?

### FALSE NAMES AND IDENTITY THEFT

Now, let's take this concept a step further. Every day people refer to diseases by name: cancer, multiple sclerosis, pneumonia, Crohn's disease, asthma—the list goes on. But when you compare these so-called names to how Jesus addressed sickness in Scripture, you see something different.

These conditions aren't true names. They are identifiers assigned to evil spirits in an attempt to give them some kind of identity. And Jesus Himself made this clear:

- In Luke 13:11, Jesus encountered a woman who had been crippled for eighteen years, but He didn't call her condition "spinal

65

deformity" or "arthritis." He called it what it was—a spirit of infirmity.

- In Mark 9:25, Jesus rebuked a deaf and mute spirit—not "hearing loss" or a "speech impediment" but the spirit causing these afflictions.

This tells us something powerful: Sickness and affliction are not identities; they are intrusions.

## THE DEVIL'S IDENTITY CRISIS

Because the devil lacks a true name, he is desperate to take on any identity he can get. This is why he readily accepts names like Lucifer or Satan, even though those were never given to him by God. Mankind was the one who labeled him, trying to assign him an identity he never truly had.

Think about it: In the Bible God is the one who names things with purpose. He names Adam, Eve, the angels, the heavens—everything He speaks a name over has meaning and divine intent. But the devil? He lost all claim to anything that carried true significance.

And because he cannot create—only counterfeit—he cannot give names either: not to himself and certainly not to anyone else.

This brings us to a final, crucial point: Names always have purpose. They represent identity, calling, and destiny. Every name spoken by God carries weight and meaning. That's why, when we truly understand this, we realize something powerful: The enemy can never define you. He can only attempt to deceive you.

No matter what label the world tries to stick to you,

your true identity can come only from the One who created you. The devil has no power over this.

And that's a truth worth holding on to.

## Mark Twain's Haunted Mansion

I lived in Connecticut for over two decades, and in a state that small, nearly everyone has visited the Mark Twain House in Hartford at least once. It's a landmark, a piece of literary history, and a common destination for families and students. Schools schedule annual field trips, and it's a well-known spot for tourists and history enthusiasts alike.

But for all its historic charm, there's something else that lingers in the mansion: a darker, more unsettling presence. Every guided tour carries with it an eerie story, a whispered legend that the mansion is haunted.

One of the most chilling accounts tour guides often share involves a security guard who patrolled the mansion at night. As he made his rounds, everything seemed fine—until he entered the basement. That's when plates were violently thrown at him, even though no one was there. He described the experience in detail: the sheer strength of the objects flying across the room, the oppressive feeling in the air, and the certainty that he was not alone.

His account was not a theatrical storytelling meant to entertain guests. It was a firsthand testimony of terror. The mansion embraces its reputation for paranormal activity. It opens its doors for special Halloween events and haunted tours, acknowledging that many believe the home is filled with restless spirits. But where did this haunting begin? And what could have invited such a presence?

Naturally, being the investigator that I am, I began asking questions. What could explain such violent disturbances? Why did so many people believe spirits roamed the Twain mansion? It didn't take long to uncover something that few people ever discuss. After researching articles, reading testimonies, and even studying Mark Twain's writings, I came across something deeply unsettling.

And honestly? It makes too much sense to ignore.

## The Unusual Names of Mark Twain's Cats

Mark Twain was widely known for his love of cats. But what many people don't realize is that he gave them strange, dark, and ominous names, including these:

- Famine
- Pestilence
- Sin
- Satan[1]

Pause for a moment and let that sink in.

We've all heard the phrase saying "If you look for trouble, you'll find it." Now imagine Twain, day after day, walking through his house and calling out these names: "Come here, Pestilence!" "Sin, where are you?" or "Satan, it's time for dinner!"

To some it may have seemed like quirky humor—a literary genius playing with satire even in the naming of his pets. But what if it was more than that? What if Twain unknowingly was inviting something into his home?

Many people dismiss the spiritual world as superstition. But for those who understand the power of words and names, there is something deeply disturbing about the idea of summoning darkness into a home, even in jest.

Could it be that Twain's habit of speaking these names aloud—over and over—opened a door for those types of spirits to pass through?

## SUFFERING IN THE TWAIN HOUSEHOLD

Looking at Twain's life, one can't help but notice the pattern of suffering and tragedy that seemed to follow his family while they lived in that mansion:

- His twenty-four-year-old daughter died from illness.

- His nineteen-month-old son died of disease.

- His wife became severely sick and stayed that way for nearly the entire time they lived there.

- He suffered devastating financial loss that nearly destroyed him.

- His famously lighthearted, adventurous writing took a dark and somber turn.[2]

The overwhelming weight of suffering became so unbearable that Twain eventually sold the house. Coincidence? Maybe. But for those who understand the spiritual realm, it's hard to ignore the possible connection between what was spoken in that home day after day and the suffering that followed.

Imagine if, instead of repeatedly saying names such as Sin, Pestilence, and Satan, Twain had spoken the names of God in his home. Imagine if, instead of calling out darkness, he had spoken life. How different would his home have been?

## THE POWER OF NAMES AND SPOKEN WORDS

Words carry tremendous power. Throughout the Bible we see that names reflect identity, purpose, and destiny. When God assigns a name, it is not random. It carries deep significance.

- Abram became Abraham, meaning "father of many nations" (Gen. 17:5).

- Jacob became Israel, meaning "one who struggles with God" (Gen. 32:28).

- Simon became Peter, meaning "rock" (Matt. 16:18).

Names are not just labels. They are declarations of purpose.

Now, contrast that with what Twain was saying daily in his home. When he repeatedly called out the names of darkness, was he unintentionally declaring something over his household?

But it's important to remember—it's apparent that the devil no longer has a real name. After the fall, the devil was stripped of his name. That's why he is only referred

*The Devil Can't Give Names*

to with titles, unlike the angels, who did not fall and were given names by God—such as Michael and Gabriel—and retained them.

He is called the accuser, the father of lies, and the prince of darkness. Nowhere in Scripture do we see God assigning him a name before the first century AD. So what does the enemy do? He takes on whatever identity he is given.

This is why he readily accepts the names people give him—satan, Lucifer, Beelzebub—because without those titles, he has nothing. He latches onto the words we speak and uses them to fuel deception.

If you name something, you claim it as such. You give it identity and authority. This is why what we say matters.

## Whom Are You Calling On?

Imagine if Twain had spoken the names of God in his home as frequently as he called on his cats. Instead of "Come here, Sin!" or "Satan, stop hiding," what if he had filled his home with the following?

- "Jehovah Jireh, my provider!"
- "Emmanuel, God with us!"
- "Holy Spirit, fill this place!"

How different would the atmosphere in that house have been?

This is why calling on the name of the Lord carries power. If you give the devil a name, he will gladly take it. But when you call on the name of Jesus, He will always answer. And where His name is spoken, His presence will dwell. That is a truth worth remembering.

Everything the devil does is a cheap imitation of God's original design. He lacks originality, authority, and the ability to name anything. Throughout Scripture you will never find an angel, fallen angel, demon, principality, or even an animal formally naming anyone or anything. That privilege is reserved only for God and mankind. Naming is not just an act of identification; it is an impartation of purpose, destiny, and authority.

From the beginning, God established naming as a divine function. He named Adam, gave Adam the authority to name the animals, and even allowed Adam to name Eve. Parents throughout Scripture were given the right to name their children. This pattern never breaks because naming is a function of authority. And since the devil lost all authority, he is incapable of naming.

We were made in the image of God, and being made in His image means we share certain aspects of His nature—not all of it but enough that we have been given dominion, free will, and the ability to create, speak, and establish.

Jesus emphasized this in the Gospels when He said, "He who believes in Me, the works that I do he will do also; and greater works than these he will do, because I go to My Father" (John 14:12). Jesus was showing us that God's power flows through us—because He is *working* through us. When Jesus physically left the earth, He handed down His authority to His followers, empowering them to carry on His work. This, in and of itself, is astonishing!

No other so-called god or deity allows its followers to do its works. False gods demand worship, sacrifice, and blind obedience, yet they do not share their power with

## The Devil Can't Give Names

their followers. But the true God? He is so powerful, so sovereign, and so secure in His glory that He allows His people to operate in His power. He works through us, with us, and in us. That is humility. That is love. No counterfeit god can ever match that.

Since the beginning of time, the devil has tried to replicate God's authority, but because he lacks the ability to create, he only counterfeits. God has divine wisdom, while satan brings false wisdom through deception. God gives identity, while satan tries to erase identity. God names, while satan labels.

The difference between a name and a label is profound. A name carries destiny. It is spoken with purpose, direction, and love. A label is a counterfeit. It is an attempt to replace identity with limitations. The devil cannot assign names because he has no original power, so instead he tries to slap false labels on people to strip them of their God-given identity. This is why the world is filled with false identities, false ideologies, and false perceptions. If the devil can't name you, he will try to make you forget who you are.

God does not operate in counterfeits, deception, or manipulation. He is the true Creator, the giver of life, the One who calls things into existence. And He holds the power to name. The Bible says in Isaiah 43:1, "Fear not, for I have redeemed you; I have called you by your name; you are Mine."

That's the difference. God calls you by name. The devil? He can accuse, deceive, and lie. But he will never hold the authority to name, create, or define.

At the end of the day there is only one voice that matters. Not the devil's lies. Not the world's opinions. Not even your own doubts. Only the voice of the One who created you. If God alone holds the power to name, then that means only He can define you. So reject the enemy's labels and hold fast to the truth: You are who God says you are. You have the identity God has given you. Your purpose is what God has spoken over you.

Everything else is a counterfeit. And counterfeits will never hold power over the real thing.

## Little Gods in a Cubby

Years ago my family and I lived in Middletown, Connecticut—which, as the name suggests, is positioned right in the heart of the state. It was a diverse community, home to people from all over the world. Many of them had come for work, and as a result, the neighborhood where our apartment was located became a melting pot of different cultures, beliefs, and traditions.

During my time there, I befriended a woman from India who practiced Hinduism. We built a friendship over time, often taking long walks together and visiting each other's homes. She was kind, warm, and welcoming, and I enjoyed learning about her culture, as much as she enjoyed asking about mine.

One day while visiting her home, I asked for a glass of water. Being the gracious host that she was, she usually would have gotten it for me, but since she was busy, she told me I could help myself. I walked into the kitchen and opened one of the cabinets, expecting to find cups or plates. But instead I was met with something unexpected.

Inside the cabinet there were no dishes, no glasses, no spices—only rows of small porcelain statues. Some were shaped like miniature people; others appeared to be animals. There was nothing else in sight. It was as though this cabinet had been reserved for something entirely different from what I had expected.

Curious, I turned to her and asked, "What are these?"

She answered without hesitation, "Oh, those are my gods."

I blinked. "Your gods?"

She nodded, smiling. "Yes, these are the gods I worship."

At that moment something stirred inside me. I love Jesus deeply, and I know how much He loves every one of us. His love is unmatched, immeasurable, and beyond anything we could ever comprehend. He doesn't just sit on a shelf—He is alive, powerful, and intimately involved in our lives.

The fact that Jesus willingly suffered the most gruesome, humiliating death imaginable just so we could have eternal life and be freed from the weight of sin is something no other god has ever done. His sacrifice was an act of immeasurable love—not distant or detached but deeply personal.

So, feeling a strong prompt in my spirit, I decided to ask my friend a simple but important question.

"So these are your gods?"

She nodded again. "Yes."

I paused and then asked, "What do they do? What have they done?"

Immediately she became animated, excited to share. She explained that one of them could cover an entire ocean with his hand. Another could pick up an entire mountain effortlessly. She went on, listing grand, supernatural feats attributed to these statues.

I listened patiently as she described all the things she believed they were capable of doing. Yet something in her words stood out to me—she kept saying what they could do but never what they had actually done.

So after she finished, I asked, "I hear you saying that these gods can do all these things, but what have they done for *you*?"

For the first time in our conversation, she hesitated. She looked at me, fumbled for words, and then paused completely. After a moment, she finally said, "Well, you see, again, he can pick up a mountain with one hand." That was all she could say.

The truth was evident: These so-called gods had done nothing for her. Her belief in them was based solely on what she had been taught, passed down through tradition. She could repeat stories about their abilities, but there was no personal connection, no real experience, and no moment where these gods had moved in her life.

It was a stark contrast to the God I know—the living God, the God who answers prayers—who moves powerfully in the lives of His people and transforms hearts, heals, delivers, and speaks.

That moment solidified something for me: Any god that is not the true God can do nothing for you.

The Bible speaks clearly about this in Psalm 115:4–8:

> Their idols are silver and gold, the work of men's hands. They have mouths, but they do not speak; eyes they have, but they do not see; they have ears, but they do not hear; noses they have, but they do not smell; they have hands, but they do not handle; feet they have, but they do not walk; nor do they

mutter through their throat. Those who make them are like them; so is everyone who trusts in them.

These man-made gods—these lifeless idols—hold no power. They do not have eyes to see, ears to hear, or mouths to speak. They are nothing more than objects created by humans and shaped from clay, wood, or stone.

## WHY WOULD ANYONE WORSHIP THE CREATED INSTEAD OF THE CREATOR?

Why would anyone put their faith in something man-made when the One who made mankind is right there, waiting with open arms?

That moment in my friend's kitchen was not just eye-opening for her—it was eye-opening for me. It made me realize how many people around the world are placing their trust in false gods—not because they have personally seen their power but because they have been taught to believe in them.

And yet these gods remain silent.

They cannot answer prayers.

They cannot love.

They cannot heal.

They cannot save.

But Jesus can. Jesus is alive. He is not a lifeless object sitting on a shelf, waiting to be dusted off. He is moving, working, and changing lives every single day.

And unlike idols He knows your name.

He sees you.

He hears you.

He loves you.

And He has already proved it in the most powerful way possible—by dying for you so you could live.

If my friend had asked me what Jesus had done for me, I would have had an endless list of answers.

- He saved me when I was lost (Luke 19:10).

- He forgave me when I didn't deserve it (Titus 3:5).

- He rescued me from darkness (Col. 1:13–14).

- He gave me peace when my heart was troubled (John 14:27).

- He healed my brokenness and restored my soul (Ps. 23:3).

My God is not silent.

My God is not motionless.

My God is alive.

And the truth is, He's not just my God—He is the *only* God.

That is why I will never bow to an idol, never place my faith in something powerless, and never forget the truth that only Jesus saves, heals, redeems, and transforms.

He is the only One worthy of worship. And the world needs to know it.

This is why I always say that for every original, there are countless counterfeits. There is only one true God, yet there are millions of false gods, false religions, false ideologies—all attempting to imitate or replace the reality of the One who created all things.

## The Devil Can't Give Names

Have you ever known anyone who copies everything someone else does? Someone who lacks their own ideas, who refuses to put in the effort to create something original but instead imitates, replicates, and claims credit for something they had no hand in producing? If you've ever experienced this personally, you know how incredibly frustrating it is. You put in the hard work, you pour your energy into something meaningful, you create something unique—only for someone else to come along, copy it, and try to pass it off as their own. It's infuriating because it's dishonest, unearned, and undeserved.

Now, take that frustration, that sense of injustice, and imagine how God must feel. This is exactly why He says, "For you shall worship no other god, for the LORD, whose name is Jealous, is a jealous God" (Exod. 34:14). Not in the human sense of jealousy, which is often rooted in insecurity, but in the righteous jealousy of a Creator who refuses to share His glory with counterfeits. He is the sole author of life, the true architect of the universe, and the One who formed the earth, the heavens, the stars, and everything within them. And yet the world is filled with cheap imitations—false gods that try to steal the credit and deceive people into worshipping something lesser, something empty, something that has no power.

But we were not made for counterfeits. Among all of creation we alone were made in the image of God. No other creature, no other being—not angels, animals, or any other living thing—bears the divine reflection of the Almighty. That means we are His most prized creation, His masterpiece, and the ones He chose to resemble Himself. Being made in His image is one of the greatest honors we could ever receive.

Think about that for a moment. The God of the universe—the One who created the galaxies, the oceans, the mountains, and the stars—looked at you and me and said, "I will make them like Me."

What higher privilege could we possibly have? There is no one above Him, and yet He placed His own reflection in us. That means we are exceptional, unique, and set apart from the rest of creation. The only thing greater is having His Spirit come to live *inside* us.

And yet, despite this incomparable truth, the enemy works tirelessly to distort it.

From the beginning satan has tried to deceive humanity into believing in counterfeits. He has convinced many that there are "other gods"—false deities and empty idols that people bow down to, sacrificing their time, their worship, and their souls. But how can the created be greater than the Creator? The irony is glaring, as even the devil himself is a created being. He did not form himself. He did not bring himself into existence. God made him.

Yet he has deceived millions into rejecting the One who created him, leading them to worship lifeless idols, false spirits, and powerless gods that cannot see, hear, or move. This is more than deception; it is a direct insult to God.

The beauty we see around us—the mountains, the oceans, the breathtaking landscapes, the vastness of space, and the miracle of life—none of it came from a counterfeit. It all bears the signature of the true Creator.

So who are we to give credit to anyone else? Who are we to attribute the glory of God's handiwork to something man-made, to something false, to something that has no power?

The truth is undeniable: There is only one God. He

alone is worthy of worship. He alone deserves glory. And no counterfeit will ever change this.

## THE DEVIL HAS ONE MISSION

Always keep in mind the powerful truth found in John 10:10, where Jesus warns, "The thief does not come except to steal, and to kill, and to destroy." This is not just a statement; it is a warning—a reminder that the devil's sole mission is to rob, corrupt, and annihilate everything that belongs to God. And if we truly understood the depths of this deception, we would be far more vigilant in recognizing the subtle traps, manipulations, and spiritual attacks that surround us daily.

The devil is not just interested in stealing God's glory; he is obsessed with taking anything that reflects God Himself. And because you and I were made in God's image, that makes us a constant reminder of everything satan has lost. Every time he looks at you, he sees the image of the One who cast him out of heaven. That alone fuels his hatred.

This is why he works so aggressively to distort, defile, and erase the divine image of God in mankind. Ever wonder why there has been such a radical push to alter, disfigure, and manipulate the human body? It is not just a passing trend; it is an orchestrated attack. The enemy wants people to look as little like God as possible. This is a direct assault on creation itself.

Never forget that we were fearfully and wonderfully made (Ps. 139:14). Our design was not accidental. It was intentional, holy, and set apart. And because of that, the devil despises it.

From the beginning his plan has always been the same: to imitate, counterfeit, and steal.

His first great deception was an attempt to hijack God's identity. In heaven he did not just seek to be like God—he wanted to *be* God. And for that he was violently cast out of heaven, stripped of his glory, and left with no true identity.

But his fall did not change his nature.

If anything it made him more corrupt, more bitter, and more determined to steal what he could never have.

And if he cannot take God's identity, he will do everything in his power to take yours.

How does he do it? The most obvious way is through demonic possession, but that's only temporary. We see this throughout history—in violent crimes and in heinous acts of evil that go beyond human comprehension. Many times, people who commit such atrocities are under the influence of demonic forces, their bodies being used as temporary vessels for destruction. And after they are used, they are discarded.

Because that's how satan works: He uses you, abuses you, and then abandons you to take the fall.

I wouldn't give him an inch. Give him an inch, and he'll take a mile. Give him a ride, and he'll take the driver's seat.

But his goal is even more sinister than demon possession.

His ultimate plan is to steal *all* of you. He doesn't just want to influence you or control you temporarily; he wants your entire being. What does that mean? He wants your soul.

I know it sounds clichéd when people say, "The devil is after your soul," or when we hear about people selling their souls to him. But this is not something to be taken lightly. It is real.

And it is not just a random act of rebellion when someone gives themselves over to darkness. For that person it is a decision that affects eternity. And to the enemy it is a victory.

Every time someone willingly hands over their soul to the devil, it is an act that grieves the heart of God in ways we cannot begin to comprehend, because your soul is precious. It is the most valuable thing you possess. And the devil knows that once he has it, he has taken something irreplaceable. This is why we must be watchful, prayerful, and unwavering in our faith.

The battle for your soul is real. And the only way to win is to remain in the hands of the One who created you, loves you, and has already defeated the enemy on your behalf.

Hold onto that truth. Never let it go.

# Chapter 6

# NO SOULS IN HELL

If Daniella had known that questioning everything she had been taught about the soul would lead to the weirdest experience of her life, she probably would've just minded her own business and kept scrolling through cat videos.

But no. She had to be curious.

Curiosity, as it turns out, has consequences.

It all started when she was at her family's weekly Sunday dinner—a chaotic event at which her mom insisted on making enough food to feed a small army. Her Aunt Regina would tell the same story about that one time she "met" Denzel Washington (which became more exaggerated every week). And her little cousins would run around like caffeinated squirrels.

Daniella was mid-bite into a forkful of mashed potatoes when her dad, a man who loved *random* theological debates, said, "Hey, you ever wonder if the soul is just your mind, will, and emotions?"

Daniella chewed slowly. "I mean...yeah? Isn't that what we were always taught?"

Her dad smirked. "Then why does Jesus say to love God with your heart, soul, *and* mind? Seems kinda redundant, don't you think?"

Daniella paused. "Huh?"

She had never thought about it. It was one of those facts she had just accepted—like how nobody knows where their stray socks disappear to or why *salmon* is pronounced with a silent *l*.

But the more she thought about it, the weirder it became. If the soul and the mind were the same thing, then why did the Bible separate the two concepts? And if they *weren't* the same thing, then what was her soul?

That night she did what any reasonable person would do when faced with an existential crisis: She went down a rabbit hole of late-night research. And by research she meant staring at her phone in the dark, reading every article, watching every video, and flipping through every Bible verse she could find.

What did she find? Well, let's just say, it wasn't comforting.

According to Scripture her soul wasn't just a bunch of emotions swirling around like a Hallmark movie inside her brain. It was her identity—the element that made her *her*. Not her career, her personality quirks, but her essence.

And that's where things got spooky.

She learned that when a person goes to hell, they lose their body and their soul and are left as just a spirit—a spirit that has full awareness, memory, and consciousness. Just...no soul.

So basically a person in hell becomes a useless, tormented nothing—a zombie, but not the cool kind.

## No Souls in Hell

Daniella sat straight up in bed. What in the horror-movie nonsense was this?

She always thought people went to hell and just... burned. For example, *Ouch, fire, bad.* But this? This was worse. This was losing yourself completely. Becoming a nameless, bodiless, identityless void.

She grabbed her pillow and screamed into it. *"Why did I look this up?"*

The next morning she was still shaken.

She walked into the kitchen, plopped into a chair, and muttered, "Did you know the soul can die?"

Her mom, without looking up from chopping onions, said, "Yeah."

Daniella squinted. "Excuse me?"

Her mom shrugged. "It's in the Bible—Ezekiel, Psalms, Matthew. The soul isn't immortal."

Daniella stared at her. "And you didn't think to mention this sooner? Like, 'Hey sweetie, hope you're having a great day. Also, your soul can die. Love you.'"

Her mom wiped her hands. "I thought you knew."

Daniella threw her hands up. "No, Mother. I did not know I was walking around with a soul that could expire like old milk."

Her mom laughed and kissed her forehead. "Well, now you do."

*Great. Fantastic.*

Now, on top of worrying about bills, traffic, and whether she had left the oven on, she had to worry about keeping her soul alive.

For the next few days Daniella couldn't stop thinking about it.

Everything she did made her wonder, "Is this affecting my soul?"

She cut someone off in traffic. *Did I just weaken my soul?*

She skipped morning prayer. *Was that a soul-level offense?*

She binge-watched reality TV instead of reading her Bible. *Was she one step closer to becoming a zombie?*

It was exhausting.

And then, one afternoon, her best friend Lucy (the only person who could handle Daniella's dramatic existential spirals) asked, "OK, but what does this mean for your life?"

Daniella groaned. "It means my soul is my identity. And if I don't protect it, I could end up losing myself entirely."

Lucy raised an eyebrow. "So...like when you spent two years in that toxic relationship and started acting like someone you weren't?"

Daniella's eye twitched. "That's not the same thing."

Lucy folded her arms. "Isn't it?"

Daniella opened her mouth—then shut it.

Lucy had a point. For years Daniella had let other people define her. She had changed who she was to fit into relationships. She had buried parts of herself to avoid conflict. She had spent so much time being who everyone else needed her to be that she had almost lost herself entirely.

And now she realized that was exactly what Jesus had meant when He said in Matthew 16:26, "For what profit is it to a man if he gains the whole world, and loses his own soul?"

It wasn't just about hell. It was about *right now*.

Every time she let the world tell her who she was instead of God, she was losing parts of her soul. Every time she prioritized people's opinions over what she knew was right, her soul took a hit. Every time she let insecurity, fear, or someone else's expectations dictate her decisions, she was handing away pieces of herself.

And if she wasn't careful? One day she would wake up and not recognize herself at all.

She grabbed her phone, opened her Bible app, and whispered, "No more."

It was time to protect her soul. Not just from hell, but from anything or anyone that tried to erase who God had made her to be.

## WHAT IS THE SOUL...REALLY?

You see, the soul is not just your mind, will, and emotions. This idea has been regurgitated in churches, social networks, Bible studies, small groups, and small conversations for years on end, but that is not what the Bible describes as the soul at all. (This is why I encourage everyone who reads this book not to take my word for anything, but rather bring what you read to the Father and ask Him for revelation.) In the end only God has the final word, and He is not a God of confusion. If what I say is true, He will confirm it. The Bible specifically says, "God hath spoken once; twice have I heard this" (Ps. 62:11, KJV).

I know it's weird to hear something that contradicts what you've heard for a long time (and possibly all your life), but in some instances, we should probably look further into a topic to find the truth.

According to Luke 10:27, the soul and the mind are two different things: "'You shall love the LORD your God with all your heart, with all your soul, with all your strength, and with all your mind,' and 'your neighbor as yourself.'" You don't have to look too closely to notice that both mind and soul are mentioned in that verse.

So now we ask, What is the soul?

Put plainly, your soul is your identity. It is who you are. It is Ashley, it is Luke, and it is everyone walking this planet at the moment. Without your identity you are a complete nobody. Your soul means everything to God because it is who you are. Your personality is all wrapped up in it. *Who* you are and *how* you think—that is who you are. But it is not your *mind*.

Jesus confirms that the soul and the mind are two separate things in Luke 10:28, when He says, "You have answered rightly; do this and you will live." The mind is paired with your spirit, which is what you are. In other words, you are a *spirit* (which can never die) that has a *soul* (which is the identity of the spirit) that possesses a body.

## No Souls in Hell

Without the soul you would merely exist. What qualifies us as bearing the image of God is that we have a body, spirit, and soul. If you were to lose your soul, you would no longer bear God's image because you would be incomplete.

When a person goes to hell, they lose their body *and* soul and become mere spirits without purpose, yet their mind is still aware of what is happening. Every one of their senses is also still in full swing, even more intensely than when they resided on earth. Consider angels, who have a soul and a spirit but don't possess a body. The devil and the fallen angels, by contrast, are spirits that lack both. This is what a person becomes when they enter hell, which confirms what Jesus said to the unbelievers: that they are like their father, the devil (John 8:44). They end up like him—soulless and bodiless.

Jesus promises us that mansions and rewards are waiting for us in heaven, which brings us to what He said in Mark 8:36: "For what will it profit a man if he gains the whole world, and loses his own soul?"

This verse isn't just reminding us of the obvious—that all the possessions you gain on earth won't mean a thing if, in the end, you die and go to hell and are left with nothing. It's also inviting us to consider what we might lose if we turn away from loving God. Because without that love, we risk becoming hollow versions of ourselves, merely going through the motions here on earth before facing—let's be honest—a hot, torturous hell with zero hopes or dreams.

Again, spirits are forever. The soul is a conditioner. It is the utmost tragedy for one to end up possessing a spirit without a soul. Nowhere does the Bible say the soul is immortal; it does, however, say the spirit is. Ezekiel 18:4 and James 5:20 make it clear that the soul can die.

This takes place in hell, according to Matthew 10:28. We also see in Numbers 16:31–35 that God opened up a hole in the earth for the wicked to fall into as a form of His judgment. Where do you think they fell *to*? More than likely, Hades, a.k.a. hell. Their bodies and souls were destroyed in that process.

When Jesus died on the cross, He descended to the chambers of hell (1 Pet. 3:19; 4:6), and Scripture tells us that he preached to the *spirits* there. It does not say he preached to the *souls*. Acts 2:27, referring to Jesus, says the Father would not leave His soul in hell. Why? Because souls can't reside there.

When referring to those who die for Christ during the great tribulation and those who refuse to take the mark of the beast, Revelation 20:4 says,

> And I saw thrones, and they sat on them, and judgment was committed to them. Then I saw the souls of those who had been beheaded for their witness to Jesus and for the word of God, who had not worshiped the beast or his image, and had not received his mark on their foreheads or on their hands. And they lived and reigned with Christ for a thousand years.

This confirms souls do exist in heaven but not in hell.

## Your Soul Is Worth It

In Scripture you will never come across an order from God, let alone a verse, that tells you to win spirits. Again,

*No Souls in Hell*

a spirit is just *what* you are, not who you are. God wants all of you. He doesn't want to see you broken into pieces—a spirit without a soul. He loves looking at you. You are the best reflection of Him.

Jesus didn't die to save your body or spirit. He died to save your soul. Your soul is the ultimate linkage to a complete body and spirit through Jesus Christ, because once He has your soul, He has your spirit and your body. The soul is the most fragile part of a triune human. Why do I say that? Because we were made in God's image and likeness. God is the Father, the Son, and the Holy Spirit all in one, and we are made the same. We are body (like the Son), spirit (like the Holy Spirit), and soul (like the Father). Yet we're one being just as He is one.

Chapter 7

# THE DEVIL'S GREATEST FEAR

The sky over the city was a mess of fading gold and deepening purple, the last traces of daylight melting into the streets below. Elias walked among the crowds, his thoughts distant, as if he existed in some space between reality and something greater. He carried within him a strange certainty that he was meant for more, but he had no proof or direction, just an unshakable sense that something had been missing his entire life.

From as early as he could remember, Elias had been different. Things came easily to him—too easily. He could fix things he had never seen before, calculate equations without even realizing he was doing it, and learn new skills as if they had always been a part of him. Where others struggled, he excelled. And yet, despite all this, he never felt whole. There was a part of him that was a mystery, locked away beyond his reach.

Raised in the foster care system, Elias had learned the hard way that life isn't kind to those without connections. He drifted through different homes and schools, never staying long enough to belong. But no matter where he went, success followed him like a shadow. Employers took notice, people whispered about him, and doors always seemed to open—until he met Malcolm Kincaid.

Kincaid was the kind of man who could make or break destinies. He owned nearly everything worth owning in the city; his empire was built on secrets, manipulation, and whispered threats. When Elias landed a job at one of Kincaid's firms, it was just another stepping stone, or so he thought.

Kincaid saw something in Elias that others hadn't. Within weeks the young man was promoted and given responsibilities far beyond his experience level. The board members scoffed, but Elias thrived, his natural instincts making him a powerhouse of efficiency and intelligence. It wasn't long before he was known as the "Golden Child," the prodigy who could do no wrong. His success baffled even him, but Kincaid was different—he wasn't just intrigued. He was *uneasy*.

Something about Elias gnawed at him. The young man was too perfect, too natural, too *familiar*. So Kincaid, a man who left nothing to chance, started digging. The deeper he went, the more uneasy he became.

And then he found it.

Elias was not just some prodigy. He was the son of *him*—the man who had once held a power so unimaginable that people spoke of him like a myth, a force that even Kincaid himself had feared. Elias's father had disappeared years ago, leaving behind only speculation, but now—now his *son* stood right in front of Kincaid, oblivious to his own legacy.

Panic set in. If Elias ever discovered the truth and realized who he was, Kincaid's entire empire would be at risk. Power like that couldn't be contained and couldn't be controlled. So Kincaid did what he did best: He manipulated.

Elias's rise came to a halt. At first it was subtle: a demotion disguised as a lateral move. "A better fit for his skills," they said. Then certain responsibilities were taken away under the pretense of "lessening his burden." Meetings took place without him, projects were reassigned, and soon the same doors that had flung open for him refused to budge.

At first Elias didn't question it. Maybe he had overestimated himself. Maybe he *wasn't* as exceptional as he had once thought. Doubt crept in; his confidence was shaken in ways it never had been shaken before. But circumstances have a way of revealing what's hidden.

One evening on his way out of the office, he crossed paths with an old man standing beneath a flickering streetlamp. There was something about the way the man stared at him—something unsettling—like he was looking at a ghost.

"You look just like him," the man finally murmured, his voice heavy with meaning.

"Like who?" Elias asked, his curiosity piqued.

The old man hesitated and then spoke a name that sent a ripple through Elias's soul. A name he had never heard, yet somehow it was familiar.

"Your father."

The words hit like a thunderclap. The world tilted. The old man spoke of a figure so powerful that even kings had once feared him. A man who had been forced into hiding, whose existence had threatened the balance of power in the world.

Elias pressed for more. "Who was he?"

The old man exhaled sharply, as if debating whether he should tell the truth. "He was more than a man. Some called him a guardian, others a force of nature. He was the one who could speak to the elements, and they would obey. Light bent to his will. Darkness fled at his command. He was the last of the true protectors of this world."

Elias felt his stomach tighten. He wanted to laugh and to call the old man crazy. But deep down he knew it was true. He had always known something was different about him. He just never knew *why*.

His father had been a supernatural being, not mythical but real. Hidden in plain sight. A force unlike anything the world had ever truly understood. And Elias? He was his heir.

The realization hit hard. Kincaid had *known*. He had worked to suppress him and to keep him from ever realizing his fullest potential. And Elias had let it happen.

No more.

Now knowing who he was, Elias began unlocking parts of himself that had long been dormant. His mind sharpened, his reflexes became faster, and his intuition was almost divine. The fog that had

*The Devil's Greatest Fear*

clouded him for so long lifted, revealing not just who he was but who he was meant to become.

And Kincaid? His days were numbered.

It didn't take long for Elias to find what he needed. Every deception, every crime, every thread that held Kincaid's empire together—Elias unraveled it all. The evidence was there, buried beneath layers of secrecy, but it was no match for someone who was finally *awake*.

By the time Kincaid realized what was happening, it was too late. His assets were seized, his influence crumbled, and the world that had once bent to his will now rejected him. He had tried to stifle greatness, to suppress a force greater than himself, but he had failed.

Elias walked away not just as a businessman or a prodigy but as something *more*. He had reclaimed his name. His legacy. His *destiny*.

And no one—*no one*—would ever take that from him again.

Elias paused at the edge of the city, the skyline stretching out before him. The air smelled different now. Cleaner. Lighter. Like a fresh beginning. He had spent his whole life searching for something he couldn't name—something just beyond his reach. Now he knew what it was.

He smiled to himself, a slow, knowing grin. He wasn't just a man anymore. He was walking in his purpose.

And this was only the beginning.

## WHAT DOES THE DEVIL FEAR?

So what is the devil's greatest fear? We know he's afraid of God. We know he's afraid of being damned to hell. But what else is he afraid of?

Just as in the short story that opened this chapter, the devil is afraid of *you* knowing how powerful you truly are. Because once you know who you are, he can no longer dismantle you. He can no longer get away with the schemes that he's been pulling off for thousands of years in your family line.

Remember the story I mentioned earlier about the woman who visited my home? I want you to recall her response when I spoke about how powerful we are in Christ and that we don't have to go through certain hardships in this life because of our identity. What happened? The woman, who went to the same church as I did, walked away and never visited my house again. Her response was a surprise, the opposite of what I thought she would do.

Do you know who your Father is? Come on now! He is the Creator of the universe. He made every cell and ligament of your body. He made every planet, and He made the universe, which is said to be expanding every single day. And He chose you and no one else to execute His mission.

Given that, do you think He wouldn't give you the tools you need to do it and win? He gave you armor. Put it on! (We're gonna go over that in the next chapter.) Every human being on this earth can have the best of the best to get through this life with warrior success! You were not made to fail. Don't take this statement lightly: You are more than a conqueror in Jesus Christ!

But here's the thing: The devil wants you to remain stupid. He wants you to be ignorant of everything that he does to keep you down. He doesn't want you to know how he works or the schemes he uses. But the deceptions he slips your way are smooth and deceitful, so you must be aware of them. If you were to know everything the devil does and how he works, you would not be complacent about getting beat down every time he comes your way. Why do you lie down in the dust when you're down? Why don't you get back up like a true warrior and fight?

The devil doesn't want you to *know* anything, but he does want you to think you are a failure. He wants you to believe that you are disease-ridden. He wants you to believe that you are nothing but a poor, useless being who is on this earth to merely exist.

But everything I just stated that the devil tries to do goes against everything that God calls us to do. The Bible says otherwise, and it is unassailable. The Bible has stood the test of time. Throughout history people have tried to burn or confiscate all the Bibles; it didn't work. When alcoholics read the Bible, they get delivered. When people on their deathbeds read the Bible, they're sometimes revived and live longer than the doctors said they would. This book brings the prodigals home, saves marriages, restores hope in the future, and casts down the devil so you can stomp on him with the sole of your foot and a smile on your face.

I truly believe that the devil is the only one the Lord will gladly allow us to take joy in defeating.

We get so angry about all the things that people do to us, but if we realize the tactics of the enemy, we know that all he does is use people to do his dirty work. He will never do it on his own because he can't. He doesn't have a body to do it *with*. So he has to find somebody who is willing and able to do his dirty work, including tempting you to do things to yourself.

But when he tempts you, all you need to do is resist the devil, and he'll flee (Jas. 4:7). This is all in Scripture. The next time he tempts you to do something, say, "Do it yourself!"

Here's what he does: He uses and abuses you. He always leaves you hanging to take the blame after he's done you dirty. The sad part is that we continue to take the bait, and it happens all over again. He's redundant, so he's predictable.

A lot of us become so flustered by little problems, unpleasant situations, or unexpected turns in life. But there are some battles that we're not supposed to be fighting. Some burdens we're supposed to give to God. I'm not saying to be complacent, lie down, do nothing, and say, "Whatever, God's got it." No. You need to give it to Him and trust Him to take control of the matter. God didn't call you or me to be lazy. We need to be ambitious and proactive in this life so we can walk out our God-given purpose.

Knowing what you're capable of—*who* you are in Christ—and the One who defeated it all leaves the devil's knees knocking! His knees knock so hard, you'd think it would cause an earthquake.

When you are in Christ, you can win every time because it's not you doing the work—it's Him. Just as King David never lost a physical battle, you never have to lose either. That's not to say that we won't have hardship or get knocked down, but someone who is already defeated

## The Devil's Greatest Fear

should never be capable of defeating you. The devil puts the *L* in *loser*.

The power that kicked him out of heaven is the power that resides in you because the One who kicked the devil out of heaven lives inside you. God loves to use you. Remember, He was the first one to use bodily possession—not the devil—and He did it in such a beautiful way. If you understood this better, you wouldn't even look at it the way you do now.

When God formed Adam out of the dust of the ground, He breathed His breath and His life into Adam's body. So in him was the breath of God.

You cannot take that lightly. The breath of God is the same breath that keeps you and me alive every day. Without the breath of God in his lungs, Adam would've been like a useless mannequin. But the instant God put His mouth to Adam's face, the whole world changed. It was never the same because God had created something He was proud of. He could say, "Look at what I created! Isn't it good?" I'm sure He said, "I made the best of the best because he looks just like Me."

But when the devil looks at you, he cannot stomach it.

He fears you because he knows your potential far surpasses his. His whole mission is to make sure that you don't know what you're capable of. As long as you never come to terms with what you're capable of and never know the advantage of the power you truly have, as stated in Scripture, the devil will always have the upper hand against you.

*You* are the biggest threat to the devil. Don't think for a minute that you are ever at his mercy.

## Chapter 8

# FIGHT! FIGHT! FIGHT!

There was once a wise and noble ruler who reigned over a vast and flourishing kingdom. Under his leadership the people never lacked, never suffered hunger, and never found themselves in need. Every citizen prospered, and whenever someone fell ill, medical care was readily available. The land thrived under his reign because this ruler was not just powerful—he was just, righteous, and deeply compassionate.

His palace was known far and wide not just for its grandeur but for the kindness and fairness with which he treated those who served him. His staff was well cared for, and his love for his people was unmatched. He was a ruler like no other—a man of unwavering integrity, ruling with wisdom beyond his years.

One day, as he walked along the narrow cobblestone roads of his kingdom, taking in the beauty of the land he governed, something caught his eye. Three children—two boys and one girl—stood by the roadside. Their clothes were worn, their faces marked with traces of hardship, and their eyes held the silent story of children who had no one to care for them.

The girl, the middle child, stood between her

brothers, her small hands gripping the fabric of her tattered dress. The ruler watched them for a moment, his heart stirring within him. He could see they were orphans, left to fend for themselves in a world that had already turned its back on them.

Something inside him shifted.

Compassion welled up in his heart.

Without hesitation he approached them, his presence commanding but gentle. He knelt to their level and looked into their weary eyes.

And in that moment he made a decision that would change all their lives forever.

He reached out his hand and said, "Come with me."

And just like that he took them in—not as servants or strangers but as his own.

He raised them in godly wisdom and knowledge, training them in every way they should go so that they would never depart from the truth. He poured everything he had into them, teaching them about honor, integrity, and the responsibilities that came with their place in his kingdom. The children thrived under his care, and they loved him deeply.

But the wise ruler knew that love—to be true—must be chosen, not forced. Although he had taken them in and raised them as his own, he wanted to give them the opportunity to choose him in return. He would not impose his will on them.

As the children entered their teenage years, the moment of decision arrived. He presented them with a choice: They could remain under his care, fully accepting him as their father, or they could choose to walk away.

*Fight! Fight! Fight!*

Without hesitation all three chose to be his children.

The joy in that moment was immeasurable. They had chosen him, just as *he* had chosen them. And because they were now royalty, they were trained even further—not only in wisdom but also in who they were, what their purpose was, and why they had to exercise caution in many areas of life.

Being the children of such a renowned and powerful ruler meant they had many allies but also many enemies.

As they grew older, the king knew the day would come when they would need to face the world on their own. The siblings were close in age, each a year apart. Once the youngest, a boy, reached eighteen, the king would give them one final test of free will.

He would send them off and let them decide for themselves whether they would return to the palace. However, he would insist that they take their armor along.

This was not just any armor—it had been prepared for them from the beginning, crafted for their protection, strength, and survival. The king had already offered them years of training, preparing them for the battles they might one day face. But there was no force or obligation—only an invitation.

At first all three children eagerly participated. They learned to put on their armor properly, understanding its weight and power. But then something changed.

As time went on, they *realized* the training was optional.

The youngest child remained diligent, never missing a session. He understood that even if the battle never came, it was better to be ready than caught off guard.

The eldest, however, gradually lost interest. He saw no immediate danger and found the idea of training tedious. He was more interested in enjoying the pleasures of life than preparing for something that might never happen.

The middle child, the girl, was somewhere in between. She attended training more than the eldest but far less than the youngest. She learned the basics, enough to hold her own, if necessary, but she didn't see the need to be fully equipped.

Over time both the eldest and the middle child forgot how to properly use their armor. They became distracted, living for the moment rather than exercising wisdom and preparing for what they might one day face.

The youngest, however, never wavered. He understood something the others did not—there might not be battle that day, but one day it would come.

The day the wise ruler had to let the children go was the hardest day of his life. He had raised them, protected them, provided for them, and loved them deeply. Every fiber of his being wanted to keep them close and to shield them from the dangers of the world outside the palace walls. But he knew that love is not truly love unless it is chosen.

## Fight! Fight! Fight!

They had to decide for themselves.

Would they return to him, fully embracing their place in his kingdom? Or would they drift away, enticed by the distractions beyond his reach?

He had given them everything they needed—not to control them but to prepare them. Every lesson, every warning, and every restriction he had placed on them had been to protect them. He longed for them to understand that.

But now it was out of his hands.

The king's men prepared everything for their departure: maps for their journey and a time frame for their possible return. They were given three years. The palace maids carefully packed their clothes, and the elder men and women—those who had spent years serving under the king—offered words of wisdom as they stepped toward the gates.

But the last and most important gift the king gave them was their armor.

Each set was custom-made and tailored perfectly to fit them. It was crafted for their protection and designed for the battles their father had warned them about.

He pleaded with them one last time, saying, "Always wear your armor. You do not know the day or the hour you will need it."

There wasn't a dry eye in the palace.

The wise ruler had done everything he could to equip them for success and the best possible life they could have. Now it was in their hands.

Would they take his guidance seriously? Or would they cast it aside in pursuit of their own desires?

As they set off on their own paths, the eldest son stood out among the three. He was handsome, charming, and well liked. People were drawn to him, and he loved the attention. He was an extrovert through and through, thriving in social circles, seeking new experiences, and immersing himself in the excitement of the world.

For several months he lived lavishly, attending celebrations, making friends, and enjoying life to the fullest. He wasn't reckless; he still held onto his father's teachings in the back of his mind—but he wasn't disciplined either.

And that was his weakness.

He did not reject what his father taught him, but he failed to live by it.

His love for the world made him careless.

And then the moment his father had warned him about came.

One evening while traveling, he unknowingly crossed paths with a group of men who were enemies of his father. These were not ordinary men. They despised everything the king stood for. They saw his children as a threat simply because of who their father was.

They watched the eldest son closely, recognizing him immediately. They saw his confidence but also his vulnerability.

And worst of all?

They saw that he had left his armor behind.

It was still in the tent where he had been staying—untouched, unworn, and unused.

*Fight! Fight! Fight!*

The men attacked.

At that moment the eldest son realized too late why his father had begged him to always wear his armor.

Without it he was defenseless.

Without it he was vulnerable.

He fought bravely, but he was outnumbered and unprotected.

And in the end he lost the battle.

And he lost his life.

Then there was the middle child, the young lady. Unlike her older brother, she was quiet, observant, and deeply introspective. She was an introvert by nature, always paying close attention to details and the world around her. While she had a kind and gentle spirit—just like her brothers—she was careful about whom she let into her life.

She made wonderful friends, but she was selective in choosing them. She valued wisdom over popularity, preferring meaningful relationships over shallow connections.

Despite enjoying her journey outside the palace, she missed home.

She often wrote letters to her father, pouring out her thoughts, her experiences, and her longing to see him again. She expressed how much she missed the warmth of the palace, the wisdom of those who had raised her, and the love that had surrounded her since childhood.

Each time the ruler received her letters, his heart swelled with joy. He wrote back, cherishing every word. Knowing that one of his children still longed for him and still held onto their bond filled him with hope.

As the years passed, she built a successful and honorable life. She was known for helping those in need, lifting up the weak, and being a beacon of kindness. Her actions reflected her father's teachings, and in many ways she carried his heart wherever she went.

But one day her path led her into danger.

While traveling through unfamiliar territory, she unknowingly crossed paths with a group of people who were enemies of the king. They were the same kind of men who had once set their sights on her older brother.

But there was one difference.

Unlike her brother she had kept her armor on.

She was prepared—at least, she thought she was.

But there was one problem.

She didn't know how to use it.

Although she had taken her armor with her, she had never fully trained in how to wield it. She had attended some training classes but not enough to master the skills. She knew the basics, but over time she had forgotten how to fight.

When the attack came, she was not ready.

Her armor protected her from immediate harm, but she had no strategy and no practiced skill to defend herself properly. She hesitated, unsure of how to counter their attacks. She had everything she needed to fight but lacked the knowledge to use it.

And because of that she was captured.

The king's enemies saw an opportunity. They had already struck him once by taking the life of his eldest child. Now they believed that capturing his daughter would break him even further.

They were wrong.

The ruler's heart was wounded but not broken.

Because unlike his eldest his daughter was still alive.

And she could still be saved.

And then there was the youngest son: a grounded, level-headed young man who never let the pressures of life weigh him down. He was calm, confident, and unshaken by fear—a trait that many admired. He did not stress over the unknown, nor did he let fear dictate his actions. Instead, he trusted in what he had been taught, walking with an assurance that made him stand out from the rest.

Like his siblings he never saw himself as superior to anyone. He treated all people with kindness, regardless of their background, status, or outward appearance. He helped the poor without hesitation, spoke to the outcast without judgment, and carried himself with humility despite his royal family.

But like his siblings he too would have his

moment of testing.

One day while traveling alone through the wilderness, he came face-to-face with the same type of enemies that had ambushed his brother and captured his sister.

Only this time it wasn't a random attack.

The enemy had been watching. Waiting. Plotting.

They had already killed one of the king's children and held another captive. Now, they believed that if they could destroy the third and final child, they could finally break the kingdom.

They had no idea whom they were dealing with. Unlike his brother, who had left his armor behind, and unlike his sister, who had forgotten how to use hers, this young man was different. He had gone through every training session, mastered every technique, and wore his armor every single day. He didn't just carry it; he knew how to *use* it.

The enemy underestimated him.

There were sixty-eight men in total. Sixty-eight trained warriors, who were armed and ready to kill.

But this young man stood his ground because he knew that his father, the ruler, was wise and great. He knew that his father had given him and his siblings the finest armor ever crafted. And most importantly he knew that as long as he used it, he would never lose a battle.

So when the attack came, he did not hesitate.

With precision and skill he fought them off one by one. He used his helmet, shield, breastplate, boots, and belt exactly as they were designed to be used. Every piece of armor had a purpose, and he knew how to wield them all.

*Fight! Fight! Fight!*

His enemies were shocked! This young man was bold, fearless, and unstoppable. It was clear to them that, unlike his siblings, he knew exactly who he was.

One had fallen because he didn't take his identity seriously. One had been captured because she wasn't prepared for battle. But this one? This one knew his authority. And he used it mightily.

By the time the battle was over, every single enemy had fallen. The young man returned home victoriously, stepping back into the palace after his long journey. His father welcomed him with joy, and the entire city rejoiced at his return. But there was still one thing left to do.

He had to rescue his sister.

With wisdom and strength he rescued her from captivity. Although she was free, she had to relearn everything she had forgotten. It was painful. But now she understood the cost of neglecting what she had been given.

As for the youngest son he never wavered from what his father taught him. He applied every lesson to his life—both in battle and in peace. He didn't boast about his victories, but he was highly favored because of his obedience and his unwavering faithfulness.

He never lost sight of who he was, whose he was, and why his armor mattered.

## Remember Who You Are

Knowing who you are, whose you are, and when to put on the full armor of God makes all the difference.

## The Devil's Greatest Fear

*Not every fight is a battle, and not every battle is a war.* But you must be ready at all times. Because when the moment comes, you cannot afford to be unprepared.

Just as Scripture warns, you must know how to use your armor and use it well. For the battle will come—and when it does, what you do with what you've been given will determine your outcome.

> Finally, be strong in the Lord and in the strength of his might. Put on the whole armor of God, that you may be able to stand against the schemes of the devil. For we do not wrestle against flesh and blood, but against the rulers, against the authorities, against the cosmic powers over this present darkness, against the spiritual forces of evil in the heavenly places. Therefore take up the whole armor of God, that you may be able to withstand in the evil day, and having done all, to stand firm. Stand therefore, having fastened on the belt of truth, and having put on the breastplate of righteousness, and, as shoes for your feet, having put on the readiness given by the gospel of peace. In all circumstances take up the shield of faith, with which you can extinguish all the flaming darts of the evil one; and take the helmet of salvation, and the sword of the Spirit, which is the word of God, praying at all times in the Spirit, with all prayer and supplication. To that end, keep alert with all perseverance, making supplication for all the saints.
> —Ephesians 6:10–18, ESV

The day you decided to be a part of the family of God, you were immediately given armor. This is something

## Fight! Fight! Fight!

we need to count as an honor. That alone should give us comfort. If you're reading this and have not yet decided to become a child of God—that is, to admit you're a sinner and sincerely believe that Jesus Christ died on the cross for your sins, rose again the third day, and will soon return for you—now is the time to do so. All you have to do is ask with a sincere heart and completely turn away from your sins. Only then will you be saved from that horrible place called hell and welcomed one day into your heavenly home, where the best gathering of family awaits you.

The armor that God speaks of in the scriptures above is not metaphoric but literal. The fact that you cannot see it doesn't mean it's not there. You can't see love, but you know when you have it; realities in the spiritual realm operate the same way because we are spiritual beings.

Go back to the part of the passage that says, "Put on the whole armor." That alone is one of the most important parts of this chapter. You can't use it if it's not on you. Remember, you are given the whole armor of God, and now it is your choice to either put it on, play around with it, or let it collect dust. It is sad to say that the last thing is the most common.

Those of us who don't understand or know the authority we have are the ones who play around with it. However, those who put it on become true threats to the enemy, for he knows that you know what you're doing. He knows that you have the best battle weapons and armor in the whole universe, and you know how to use them. Like I said, you can't use it if you don't put it on.

God is a purposeful God. Therefore, every piece of armor that He's giving you is extremely effective and works every time. Did you know that every piece of armor mentioned in the scripture above is used for defense except one? That means we possess only one offensive weapon (that is, a weapon intended to attack), and you're about to find out what that is.

First, you're presented with the belt of truth. Using this provides you with unwavering support to help you stand on the truth. A lot of deception will be thrown your way, and this belt will prevent you from falling for the devil's schemes.

Second, you have the breastplate of righteousness. This is what keeps you morally on the right path. How many well-known Christian figures have we seen fall due to immorality? Some people, unfortunately, claim to have lost their faith because of the actions of these individuals. This is why the breastplate of righteousness must always remain on.

The third piece of armor is the shoes of the gospel of peace, which are on your feet. This equips you to be steadfast and ready to proclaim the gospel.

Fourth, you have the shield of faith, which is another defensive weapon. This protects you from the devil's attacks—a protection we can all relate to and recognize as something needed every hour of every day. Whatever dart is thrown your way, it can be stopped in Jesus' name!

Then, you have the fifth piece of armor, which is the helmet of salvation. This is extremely important because it protects the mind. I've noticed that the number one method the devil uses to attack believers and nonbelievers alike is thoughts. Think about how one thought can change your whole mood. One thought can change one action, which could transform your life forever. It'll change the way you see people, life, and God, if you

*Fight! Fight! Fight!*

allow the enemy to have his way through your mind. In America and other parts of the world, we see that there is a huge issue with what is called mental illness. By reading this book, you should know by now that it is merely an attack of the devil. Whatever diagnosis is given is just the description of the evil spirit hiding behind it. The mind is the best computer on this planet, which is why the devil tries so hard to knock down the firewall that God has given you and infect it with a virus. So the mind must be protected.

Finally, number six is the sword of the Spirit. This is the one you've been waiting for; it's the only *offensive weapon* that God has given you. The sword of the Spirit is the Word of God. This is why God says to write it on your heart, so even if you don't have a Bible with you, you will be able to recite it. Because when you recite scripture and speak it with authority, the devil can't stand it. He has to flee. It burns his and all his little minions' ears. I've even known people who said that when they use the Word of God against them, demons disappear into a vapor.

I think it's cool that God gives us six pieces of armor, as six is often regarded as the number representing mankind. I don't think He did this mistakenly. No other spirit or species can wear it, except for us!

Many people believe the Bible is just a great book, but it is so much more than that. It truly is a weapon.

I'm gonna share a story with you that changed my life forever.

## You Can't Fight the Devil with Fear

When my kids were small, I would always pray with them before they went to bed, and then my husband and I would pray together in our room before falling asleep. One time, however, in the middle of the night, I felt a dark presence in our room. I had fear, which I should not have had because that was not a piece of the equipment that God gave me. (So I should not have picked it up.) The presence in my room was so evil and dark that I went into the hallway leading to my children's room to pray over them again and see whether the presence was there as well. When I went into their room, I noticed that everything felt light. There was no heaviness. There was no darkness, nor was there any evil in that room or the hallway.

But when I went back into my own room, the sense of evil was so thick I could have cut it with a knife. I began to rebuke the devil out loud in the name of Jesus, but it did not work because I was saying it with fear. You can't fight the devil with his own weapons and expect to win. He knows his weapons far better than you do, and when you use them, the equipment in your hands is always a grenade against you.

So I did what I knew to do best: I opened my Bible, knelt down, and read the words in red out loud. The instant I began to read the words in red, which are the words of Jesus Christ, everything in the room *immediately* decimated in the blink of an eye. That's the power of the Word of God. So memorize scripture! This is what the Bible talks about. It's not enough to own the Bible, nor is it enough just to read it. We must *memorize* it and write it in our hearts. If you have an issue with your memory, that's

*Fight! Fight! Fight!*

no problem. Just ask the Lord to etch it on your heart, and you will never forget it once it is there.

## ETCHED ON YOUR HEART

I once had an aunt named Ruth. She was a sweet woman—the kind who never forgot your birthday and always mailed a crisp bill from Maryland to remind you she was thinking of you. As a child those are the memories that stick with you. What stood out about Aunt Ruth wasn't just her kindness or generosity; it was her unwavering love for Jesus.

As she aged, Alzheimer's crept in, stealing pieces of her memory one by one. It was heartbreaking to watch. She began forgetting names and faces, even those of the people closest to her. But the one thing she *never* forgot was Jesus. You could mention His name, and suddenly her eyes would light up. She would start talking about Him as if He had just been in the room with her five minutes earlier. She could recite scripture flawlessly, recount Bible stories with perfect clarity—but ask her who had just visited her that morning, and she would draw a blank. It was almost as if the disease had erased everything *except* Him.

That stayed with me. If I could choose what I want permanently engraved on my heart and mind, it's the Word of God. Because no matter what happens—sickness, trials, or attacks from the enemy—His Word remains. Like Aunt Ruth I want to be so rooted in Jesus that even if my mind forgets everything else, my spirit *never* lets go of Him.

Now, there are plenty of people—even some ministers—who will say, "It's not that serious" or "You don't need to go that deep." Let me tell you something: It is that serious.

We're in a battle whether we like it or not, and the devil thrives on what we don't know.

Think about it. If you don't know you have armor, you won't use it. If you don't know how to wield the weapons God has given you, you'll never fight back. And if you don't realize that you have full authority over the devil, he will *absolutely* take advantage of you, and he will keep doing so until the day you leave this earth. Ignorance isn't just dangerous; it's an open invitation for the enemy to wreak havoc in your life.

The Bible tells us that everything done in darkness will eventually come to light (Luke 8:17). So why do you think the devil operates in the dark? He doesn't want you to know what he's up to. He doesn't want you to recognize your power. He wants you stumbling around, unsure, unarmed, and unaware. Because the moment you realize who you are in Christ—the moment you put on that armor and actually use it—is the moment you become a serious threat to him.

Now, imagine this: What if every single believer truly understood their authority in Christ? What if we all put on our armor every day, ready for battle? What if we *all* fought back instead of staying on the defensive? This world wouldn't just look better; it would look completely different.

We weren't created to lose. We weren't made to sit back and take whatever the enemy throws at us. We were designed to conquer. And it's time we started living like it.

## Sight & Sound Plays

When we lived on the East Coast, one of our favorite family traditions was our annual road trip to Sight & Sound Theater in Lancaster, Pennsylvania. If you've never been there, think of it as the Christian version of Broadway—but honestly, it's way better and far more captivating. The moment you step inside, you're hit with a warm, inviting aroma that somehow makes you feel both excited and at home all at once. It's the kind of place that pulls you in, making you want to explore every corner before the show even starts.

Every year Sight & Sound puts on a spectacular production based on a story from the Bible. Over the past forty or so years, we've seen almost every one of them. My all-time favorite has always been *Joseph*. I'm not the kind of person who cries at movies or sentimental moments, but that play was an exception. I sat there, fully prepared to just enjoy the show, and before I knew it, my face was wet. No warning. No buildup. Just full-blown waterworks.

A couple of years ago, we went to see *David*, and let me tell you—it was right up there with *Joseph*. The production was powerful, but what struck me was how it highlighted a simple but crucial truth: Every time King David and the people of Israel put God first and trusted Him to lead them into battle, they always won. Not just sometimes. Not just when the odds were in their favor. Every single time.

And here's the kicker: They didn't just sit back and wait for victory to fall into their laps. They still had to put in the effort, step onto the battlefield, and do their part. But the moment they trusted God and moved forward in faith,

He took care of the rest. King David was relentless in seeking God's guidance. He didn't make decisions blindly or based on his own strength. He expected God to show up, and God *always* did.

That play left me thinking. How often do we try to fight our own battles without asking God to lead the way? How many victories do we miss out on simply because we don't trust Him enough to take charge? David's life wasn't perfect—far from it—but his success was rooted in something unshakable: his pursuit of God's heart.

That's what stuck with me the most. It wasn't just a play; it was a reminder. When we put God first and trust Him in the middle of the fight, we're never on the losing side. All we have to do is step forward, and He'll take care of the rest.

One night as I was lying in bed, I found myself deep in 1 Samuel, soaking up every word like a sponge. The more I read, the more I saw how much David clung to God. It wasn't just devotion; it was complete dependence. It was the kind of closeness that's rarely seen today, although you catch glimpses of it in some people.

Then as I kept reading, something struck me: Look at how the father figures in David's life treated him. His own father, Jesse, barely acknowledged him. When the prophet Samuel came to anoint one of Jesse's sons as the next king, Jesse didn't even bother calling David into the house. It was as if he didn't consider him important enough to be included.

Then there was his older brother. Just as David was about to step up and fight Goliath, his brother tried to crush his spirit by accusing him of being prideful, nosy, and out of place. But David wasn't there for recognition.

*Fight! Fight! Fight!*

He wasn't seeking approval. He simply wanted to glorify God because he knew God would fight for Israel.

And then came King Saul. At first Saul took David in like a son, showed him favor, and treated him like family. But as soon as David's victories started outshining his own, Saul's love turned into a dangerous jealousy. The man who once welcomed David into his palace became the one trying to take his life.

As I sat there, mulling over everything, a thought rose in my heart.

"Was David so close to You because—"

Before I could even finish the sentence, God interrupted me.

"Yes."

I blinked. That was fast.

I let the weight of that answer sink in. "Wow. That makes so much sense."

The full question I had meant to ask was "Was David so close to You because he didn't have a good father or father figure on earth?"

And the answer was obvious. God *was* David's Father. Not just in a spiritual sense—David truly saw Him as a father. He depended on Him, trusted Him, leaned on Him for guidance, protection, and identity. In return God loved David like a son, treated him like a son, and favored him like a son.

The reality is that so many people today grow up without good fathers or father figures. And then there are those who are blessed with amazing dads who love them well. But no matter what our earthly circumstances are, we have to come to a place where we truly see God for who

He is: our *Father*. The way He loved David as a son is the same way He loves each of us as His sons and daughters.

The difference is that David understood it. He respected and adored his heavenly Father the way a child should. And maybe that's why he walked in such close, unshakable favor.

After interviewing countless guests on my podcast, *The Deep Believer Show: The Normalcy of Miracles, Signs, and Wonders,* I've noticed a pattern. Those who grew up without fathers often seem to have a closer relationship with God the Father than those who had strong father figures in their lives. It was almost as if the absence of an earthly father made them lean even more into their heavenly one.

Knowing who we are is important, but knowing who God is? That's even bigger. Because if we don't truly know who He is, how can we possibly understand who we are? He is our Father. And a good father *always* fights for his children.

Growing up, my sister and I never felt unsafe—not once. We knew that if anything went down, our dad would be there in a flash, ready to defend us. I think he secretly believed he was Batman. If he so much as heard a strange noise in the middle of the night, he would leap out of bed like a ninja, checking every door and window with a sense of urgency. If we were ever in danger, he would be our personal bodyguard.

That's exactly how God is with us, especially when we have a close relationship with Him. He's not a distant figure in the clouds; He's an active, ever-present Father who rushes to our side at the first sign of trouble.

What set David apart from everyone else wasn't just his

bravery or his victories—it was his *relationship* with God. David knew God as his Father. And when David spoke, God answered. Even in the Psalms, during those moments where David felt abandoned, he always came back to the same truth: *God is with me.* He never ended a psalm in despair. He always found his way back to giving God the glory.

That's the kind of trust we need to have.

So don't be afraid to pick up your weapons and fight. Don't be afraid to put on your armor. It's not a suggestion; it's a command. When you wear it, you don't need to cower in fear, because the devil isn't stronger than you. That shouldn't even be a question.

Wearing the armor of God means you fully expect your Father to show up for you. However, you have to do your part. Sitting around talking about it won't get you anywhere. We have too many people reading the Bible and not enough people living it. That's why Scripture says to be doers of the Word, not just hearers (Jas. 1:22).

God says He will fight our battles, but notice He never tells us to leave the battlefield. He never tells us to take off our armor.

We are an army. Scratch that—we are the army of God. And we cannot afford to have any weak links. So let's band together, stand our ground, and fight every battle in the name of Jesus. Because now we know exactly who our God is—and exactly who we are.

Chapter 9

# DON'T DANCE WITH THE DEVIL

The banquet hall shimmered with gold and maroon drapes. There were silk cushions on every chair and long tables overflowing with plates of biryani, paneer butter masala, and sweets glistening with silver foil. Hundreds of guests, draped in embroidered saris and tailored sherwanis, moved like waves through the massive hall. The sound of sitars played softly in the background as waiters balanced silver trays of steaming samosas and mango lassi.

This was the biggest event of the year. Not a wedding or a festival—just a grand evening hosted by a wealthy family who, for years, had made it a tradition to invite everyone: from their business partners to the local politicians and even to the occasional Bollywood star who happened to be in town.

Seated near the front was a well-respected family: a couple with their two children, who were both in their twenties. They were known to be deeply religious, attending every festival, fasting when required, and giving generously to charities. The mother, draped in an elegant red sari, kept whispering prayers under her breath, as she adjusted her gold bangles. Her husband sat with his arms crossed, nodding respectfully at the men around him but saying little. Their children, however, were restless.

The elder, a son, had changed over the years. He had grown impatient with his family's traditions, rolling his eyes whenever his mother studied her Bible or muttered blessings before meals. "Faith is good for the weak," he often said. "The real world runs on power and money."

His sister, younger by only two years, had always looked up to him. She admired his confidence, his charisma, and his intelligence. But something about him had changed recently, and she could sense it. He had become distant—his words sharper and his presence heavier. He wasn't the brother she had grown up idolizing.

As the evening progressed, the host of the banquet made his way to their table. He was a tall, elegant man with a voice as smooth as silk. People whispered about him—how his wealth had tripled in just a few years, how he seemed to know everyone important, and how every business deal he touched turned to gold. But no one could quite explain where his fortune had come from.

He greeted the family warmly, his smile wide, but his eyes were cold. "Ah, welcome," he said, his voice filled with a practiced charm. "It is an honor to have you here tonight."

The young man smiled back, shaking his hand firmly. "I've been looking forward to this," he said.

The sister watched as her brother and the host engaged in conversation, leaning in as if sharing secrets. The laughter between them sounded

## Don't Dance with the Devil

genuine, but something about it sent chills down her spine.

After a while the host leaned in even closer. "I hear you are an ambitious man," he said, his voice dropping slightly. "You are not like the others."

The young man smirked. "I like to think so."

The host nodded approvingly. "Then let me introduce you to some very...influential people tonight."

The girl's heart pounded. She wasn't sure why, but something about this felt wrong.

Throughout the evening she noticed her brother being ushered into deeper conversations and surrounded by men who seemed different from the usual business crowd. Their smiles were too perfect and their laughter was just a little too rehearsed. The more they spoke, the more her brother seemed to lean in, intrigued, engaged—drawn in like a moth to a flame.

And then, at one point, she saw it.

One of the men pressed something into her brother's hand: a small, black card. She couldn't see what was on it, but whatever it was made her brother's face light up with interest.

She turned to her mother. "Did you see that?"

Her mother shook her head, still focused on the conversations at their own table.

As the night went on, her brother drifted further from the family, whispering with his new "friends," nodding eagerly at their words. He was laughing more than usual, and his posture was different—proud, almost arrogant.

It was as if the people around him were pulling him into something deeper, something unseen.

Then came the moment she would never forget.

One of the men leaned in close to her brother and said something she couldn't hear. Whatever it was, it made her brother's expression change instantly. His smirk faded. His eyes darkened.

He hesitated.

And then, for the first time that night, he looked back at his family.

At his mother, who was praying.

At his father, who was silent but observant.

At her—his sister—staring at him with an expression of worry and pleading.

Something in that moment seemed to break.

His grip on the black card loosened. His posture shifted.

The host, noticing the change, placed a firm hand on his shoulder. "Are you sure you are ready for this?"

For a brief moment the young man looked conflicted.

And then as if waking from a dream, he let out a breath, dropped the card on the table, and pushed his chair back. "I should go," he said, his voice slightly unsteady.

The host's smile flickered.

For the first time that evening, the warmth in his expression vanished.

But the young man didn't wait for a response.

*Don't Dance with the Devil*

He turned on his heel and walked away—back toward his family.

His sister exhaled, relief washing over her.

The banquet continued. Laughter, music, and conversations filled the hall.

At the far end of the table, the host simply watched, his fingers drumming against the polished wood.

His smile returned, but this time it didn't reach his eyes.

The young man didn't know it yet, but the devil never takes rejection lightly.

And the dance was far from over.

The young man walked briskly toward his family, toward what he couldn't quite name but knew he had almost lost. His pulse was still racing. He didn't understand what had just happened—why he felt such an intense pull toward those men or why that black card in his hand had felt like something much heavier than just paper. But one thing he did know was that he needed to get away from that table.

His sister was waiting, her face a mixture of

relief and fear. She grabbed his arm as soon as he reached her. "We need to leave," she whispered urgently.

His father, silent but always watchful, had been observing the entire evening. He didn't ask any questions. He simply nodded. "Let's go."

As they made their way toward the exit, the music in the banquet hall seemed louder, the chatter hollower. The laughter rang false. It was as if the entire atmosphere had changed, or maybe he was just seeing it clearly for the first time.

He stole one last glance at the host. The man was still seated, swirling a glass of something dark, with his lips curved into an expression that wasn't quite a smile. The men around him—the ones who had seemed so powerful, so untouchable—were watching too. But they no longer looked inviting. They looked...disappointed.

Disappointed in *him*.

The young man shuddered and turned away.

Outside, the cool night air hit him like a slap. The banquet hall, grand and illuminated, stood behind them like a palace of illusions. But here, under the vast sky, everything felt clearer.

His mother finally spoke. "What happened in there?"

He opened his mouth, but the words wouldn't come. How could he explain that he had nearly been pulled into something he didn't fully understand? That, for a moment, the world at that table had seemed more real than anything else? That he had almost chosen...what, exactly?

He ran a hand through his hair, exhaling. "I—I

don't know," he admitted. "But it wasn't right."

His sister, still gripping his arm, nodded. "I felt it too."

His father placed a firm hand on his shoulder. "You were being tested," he said quietly. "And you walked away."

The words settled over him like a blanket.

Yes. He had walked away.

As they climbed into the car, something in him whispered that this wasn't over.

The devil doesn't take rejection lightly.

And once you've started the dance, he'll always try to pull you back onto the floor.

But this time the young man knew the steps.

And he wasn't planning to dance again.

## Master Deceiver

While you're dancing with the devil, he's planning your assassination. We've all heard the saying that one of the devil's greatest deceptions is making us believe that he doesn't exist. And that's a factual statement.

Some of us have gone through life seemingly scot-free. No life is perfect, but some could testify that theirs have been pretty close. I've found that many who haven't experienced hardships or trials are the ones who are easier for the devil to deceive, in a way. They haven't seen or experienced the evil warned about in Scripture. Are they likely to look for a savior if they don't even see that they need saving from anything? That is a deception of the devil.

I knew a person who loved God to the core of her being.

She loved talking about Jesus constantly, and nothing you would say could ever shake that. But remember, the devil studies us, according to Scripture, and finds ways to see whether he can break through any cracks that may exist in our souls. One day she began to be more "open-minded" and make friends with people who didn't think or believe like her. She wanted to see how other people from other walks of life lived as well. You could call it "getting her feet wet." Gradually she began to talk less and less about God and embrace the ways of the world more. She became secular and spent her time in places where no Christian should be if they don't want others to stumble.

Her Christian relationships began to shrink as her secular friendships grew. She had become someone I'd never known—the person she was before getting saved. She began to do a slow dance with the devil, and she did not even know it. As she did, almost every aspect of her life began to crumble. This included her finances, her family, her life, her health, and her relationship with God. It took many hardships for her to turn away from the lustful desires of the world and dedicate the rest of her life back to the Lord. If she had continued down that track, the devil would have used her until he couldn't use her anymore and then orchestrated a final blow. I believe that because she knew the Lord and did not completely leave Him, the Lord restored everything to her sevenfold.

Now picture a young man who finds himself drawn to a mentor—someone who offers him guidance, a sense of purpose, and the kind of belonging he never knew he needed. For the first time he feels seen, valued, and understood. This mentor encourages him to explore new ideas: concepts that seem harmless, even intriguing. Practices such as manifestation, tapping into "hidden knowledge," and unlocking so-called spiritual enlightenment. After all, everyone seems to be doing them these days. Social media is flooded with them, self-help books praise them, and they all promise power, control, and a deeper understanding of the universe.

At first it feels good. It feels *right*. But over time something shifts inside him—something heavy, something unsettling. It's hard to explain, but it lingers. A strange weight presses on him, and an unshakable unease creeps into his nights. Sleep no longer comes easily. An unspoken fear settles in, gnawing at the edges of his mind and making him question everything.

And without even realizing it, his faith begins to slip. It's subtle at first; he skips prayer here and there, neglects reading his Bible, and shrugs off church. He tells himself he's simply evolving, expanding his mind, and embracing "truths" beyond what he once believed. What feels like self-discovery is leading him into something far more dangerous: *spiritual bondage*.

What he doesn't see is that he's not gaining power; he's losing it. He's not being enlightened; he's being deceived. The enemy never shows up with horns and a pitchfork. He shows up offering knowledge, success, and self-empowerment, all while leading people further away from the One who holds true power.

The stories above are just glimpses into the enemy's playbook—tactics he's been using for centuries to keep people from stepping into their God-given authority and identity. His goal is simple: to distract, deceive, and destroy.

If the enemy had managed to keep all these people trapped in their strongholds, they never would have fulfilled their purpose. They never would have finished the race Paul speaks of in 2 Timothy 4:7: "I have fought the good fight, I have finished the race, I have kept the faith."

Because at the end of the day, that's what this battle is about—*finishing the race*. And the only way to do that is to know who you are, whose you are, and how to walk in the truth that sets you free.

## No Celebrities on the Mission Field

One of my favorite people in the Bible is Enoch. I've always wondered, especially as a child, what made him so special that he never had to see death and could take a stroll with God to heaven. It wasn't until I opened the Book of Jasher, a book mentioned multiple times in Scripture, that I found out a possible reason.

The Holy Bible frequently touches on the person Enoch, but the Book of Jasher gave me a little bit more insight into who he was and what he was like. I want to focus on that last part. It describes Enoch as walking so close to God that he would gradually leave everything and spend time with Him. At first it would be a day alone with Him, away from everyone else. Then it went on for a week, and then eventually it became months and even years. It was all about God with him. He didn't allow himself to be sidetracked by unnecessary distractions. It was just him and God. The way of the world and the popularity that he could have taken advantage of were not his concern. He simply wanted to be with God and to please Him. Enoch was truly righteous and thus was granted a death-free journey to heaven, where he's been spending even more time with God.

Nowadays we're seeing so much corruption in the body of Christ, which is the church, that it is truly and utterly heartbreaking. The truth of the matter is that most of the evangelists, ministers, or Christian entertainers we know so well started off with pure hearts. Many of them just wanted to sing for God. Many of them just wanted to preach the gospel. Many of them just wanted to demonstrate the love of God. And God honors and loves such devotion from the core of His being. That's what puts a smile on His face.

The problem is that they allowed themselves to dance with the devil. Remember, the enemy is deceitful and cunning. He won't walk in on you and say, "Hey, I'm the enemy! Let me take you on a joyride across the dance floor so I can instruct you how to dismantle your walk with God!" He comes in subtly, and unfortunately this is what we're seeing now.

Lust, money, and fame are what eventually lured people in. And with that comes competition and status. The enemy makes it sound so sweet at first, and he may even use your loved ones to plant subtle seeds of temptation in your ear ("You deserve it!"). You eventually take the bait, but when it is no longer about God and more about who sees you, the world will not be able to see God in you. They just see...you.

Here's the thing: We must learn to want to be not famous but productive. When we fall into the trap of fame, it always becomes about "Me. Me. Me." For a while you may think the accolades are from God. However, success must be paired with a walk with God—not a dance with the devil.

I'll never forget when I started my first year in high school. I was a big introvert, and people slowly began recognizing me in the hallways. Not many people tried to hang out with me at the time. No one cared to truly befriend me, nor was my name being yelled down the halls as many were. I was just...Jenny.

One day toward the end of the year, out of nowhere, I heard my name being yelled down the school hallway: "Jenny Jones! Jenny Jones!" (Jones is my maiden name.) It wasn't just one person either but several! I was truly shocked that someone was calling my name. What had I done for so many people to suddenly start caring who I was? I couldn't figure it out. However, I soon realized that I didn't like it. These people wouldn't have given me the time of day last week. They wouldn't have waved to me passing by, but suddenly schoolmates wanted to hang out with and befriend me?

It was then that I realized that popularity is man-made. As quickly as the world can "love" you, it could end up despising you. Jesus is the perfect example. He became popular not because He was seeking it but because of who He was, how He was, and what He did for the people. Even though He was famous, He never sought fame. It came with the territory. He was never boastful or prideful. After reading about Enoch, I could easily say the same about him. He was neither prideful nor boastful, and he didn't seek fame or recognition.

That sadly has become the scope of modern-day Christianity. So many people want to be "somebody," not realizing that they have been somebody from before God

*Don't Dance with the Devil*

formed them in their mother's womb. Our mission should always be focused on Jesus Christ—always! It's not about us.

Remember, we are the created. We are the work of God's hands, and He is behind every blessing that we possess; therefore, He alone receives the recognition. We must refuse to allow the spotlight to shine on us and remain only in Christ.

When you look at those who have experienced fame, you see how so easily and quickly it leads to worship. This is evident in the secular and nonsecular worlds alike. However, we weren't created to receive worship. We can't handle it. Not even one of us can.

The popularity, fame, and worship were handled perfectly by only one person: Jesus Christ. He handled them by often drawing away from the crowds to be alone with His Father and pray. If you were to ask anyone who has achieved any level of fame, they would admit that it sometimes becomes too much to handle.

I tell my children that it's OK to admire celebrities but to never allow it to turn into worship, because, at the end of the day, they're just normal people like you and me. The only difference is that they always have cameras in their faces (and, let's be honest, often deeper pockets).

The point is that worship should always be reserved for God. You should never allow yourself to put anyone—including your pastor—so high that you think they're incapable of falling, because they can. How you view them after their fall often doesn't have to do with them. In your mind, you have placed them in God's position—a place forever unattainable for them—when, in reality, they are merely men and women.

## Children Know, so Listen to Them

I know a family who always went to church together in the 1990s. The father was the assistant pastor of the church and had a lot of responsibility. He and his wife had two daughters. The church was on the smaller side, so everyone knew one another. It was as if the community were a family.

This church was charismatic! There was never a dull moment in each service, as miracles, signs, and wonders were common. Both daughters saw these things happen and were so amazed that they could not possibly doubt God or who He is.

Eventually the pastor began to believe that he was the one performing the miracles and the wonders. He even reached the point where he shouted over the pulpit to the congregation that God didn't need them and that He had better things to do than to worry about them. He began to make bold statements, saying, "God didn't do this; I did! I'm the one who put in the work!" Members of the church gradually began to treat him as if he were a god, not even realizing they were doing so. It was as if he could do no wrong in their eyes. They were submissive to him and did whatever he requested.

It baffled the younger daughter, who was around ten years old at the time. On one December evening, she said to her father, "Daddy, this isn't right. We need to leave the church. This pastor is bad. You should leave. It's a cult."

Her father scolded her sharply and yelled in her face, "Don't speak against God's anointed!"

The girl ran to the church's exit door with tears streaming down her face. She was confused why her father refused to consider anything she had said. It came from her heart, and she knew what she expressed was true. She questioned why she was the one being punished.

A few years later the girl's father was offered a new job out of state, and he happily took it. The church sent him away with tons of gifts and even threw him a party. But a year after his relocation, no one from the church had been in touch. At that point a woman who attended the church informed him that one Sunday the senior pastor had instructed everyone never to speak to the assistant pastor again. He said the assistant pastor was a traitor for leaving, and he convinced the congregation that he was now the enemy.

In the end his ten-year-old daughter had been right.

This is only one of many stories like this that I could tell you. Children have a unique discernment about many things that we adults lack. When they speak—listen. When they warn you about certain things—listen. They often see what we no longer do, as they're often still sensitive to the spiritual realm. Children know more than you think.

## Chapter 10

# GOLD IN YOUR POCKETS

New York City. The land of opportunity, overpriced coffee, and people who will step over a man having a breakdown to make their subway train on time.

The city was alive as ever that morning—horns blaring, tourists gawking, and hot dog vendors shouting their deals as if they were on the trading room floor. In the middle of it all was one particular individual: He was an ordinary believer but one who took the Bible quite literally. That's when the situation became truly intriguing.

This wasn't just any day; this was about to be one for the books.

It all started in a little corner deli on Fifth Avenue: the kind of place where the cashier knew your name if you came in often enough, the bagels were the real deal, and the coffee was strong enough to wake the dead.

Literally. (Actually, not really.)

Right as the morning rush was starting to slow down, the door flung open with a bang. A man stormed in with his face covered by a cheap ski mask. He waved a gun in the air and shouted, "Everybody down! Hands where I can see 'em!"

Customers screamed. The cashier looked like he was about to pass out. A businessman in the corner tried to discreetly text the word "help" to his group chat.

Right there, in the middle of the chaos, someone stood.

Not ducking. Not cowering. Standing.

The robber whipped his head around, pointing the gun straight at him.

"You deaf? I said *down!*"

This wasn't just any ordinary person; this was someone who had read Mark 16:17–18 that morning and decided to believe every word of it.

Instead of fear, something else rose up. A boldness that made absolutely no sense in the natural.

The brave man lifted a hand and shouted, loud and clear, with authority, "In the name of Jesus, put the gun down."

New Yorkers have seen a lot. They've seen street performers light themselves on fire, subway preachers go on apocalyptic rants, and men in business suits sprinting after taxis as if their lives depended on it. But this? This was something new.

The air in the deli shifted.

The gunman hesitated. His hands started shaking. His breathing grew heavy.

And then—*bam!*

The gun clattered to the floor. He dropped to his knees as if he had been hit by an invisible force. He clutched his head, groaning, his body trembling like a man under a power he couldn't understand.

## Gold in Your Pockets

"I...I can't move," he stammered. "What's happening to me?"

That's when it hit him—literally. The presence of God came crashing down like an unseen wave, filling the tiny deli with something stronger than fear.

People gasped. The businessman stopped texting. The cashier stopped looking as if he might faint; instead, he now looked as though he wanted to start praying.

And then came the second miracle.

In all the commotion, no one had noticed that an elderly woman near the cold drink section had collapsed. The shock of the robbery attempt must have been too much—she had gone down instantly, her frail body lifelessly lying on the tile floor.

A younger woman crouched beside her, sobbing. "She's not breathing! Someone call an ambulance!"

Our fearless believer was already moving.

"No need."

Now, let's pause.

This is where most people would have panicked. This is where logic would have said, "Step back and let the professionals handle it." However, when you take Jesus at His word and believe He meant what He said about raising the dead, you don't let logic get in the way.

He knelt, placed his hands on the woman's chest, and took a deep breath.

"In the name of Jesus," he commanded, "get up."

Nothing.

The deli was dead silent.

A nervous cough. Someone shuffled.

And then—

The woman gasped.

As if she had been yanked back into her body, she inhaled sharply, sat straight up, and stared with wide eyes.

The deli erupted into absolute chaos.

Screams. Applause. Someone dropped their coffee. A guy in the corner fainted harder than the old woman had.

The old woman blinked, looking around. "What in the world—"

"You were dead," the young man said, hugging her and sobbing. "You weren't breathing! I thought...I thought we lost you!"

"Dead?" The old woman frowned, touching her chest. "Well, I feel great! Actually I feel better than great. My arthritis isn't hurting anymore. Is that pastrami sandwich still warm?"

At that point the cashier finally found his voice.

"What...what just happened?"

The police arrived shortly after. Two officers stormed in, expecting to take down an armed suspect, only to find the gunman still kneeling on the floor, weeping.

"I was gonna do something terrible," he confessed, his voice shaking. "But...I don't know what happened. It was like...like something stronger than me told me to stop."

One officer raised an eyebrow. "That's called getting caught, buddy."

"No, you don't understand!" the robber insisted.

"I felt it! The second he said the name—" He pointed at the believer—"something hit me. I...I couldn't fight it! I saw my whole life flash before my eyes. I saw every bad thing I ever did. And then—" He choked up. "And then I felt love. Like real love, for the first time ever. I...I don't want this life anymore. I don't wanna steal. I don't wanna hurt people. I want whatever he has."

The deli fell silent again.

The cops exchanged glances.

One of them shrugged. "I mean...we were gonna arrest him, but, uh...I don't know what to do with this."

The believer smiled. "I do."

And right there—inside a tiny New York deli, surrounded by bagels, spilled coffee, and a crowd of awestruck New Yorkers—the robber gave his life to Jesus.

By the time the sun set, the entire city seemed to be buzzing with the story.

The deli cashier told every customer who walked in that day.

The businessman who tried to text for help sent a company-wide email about what had happened.

The elderly woman, who now felt younger than ever, told the whole assisted living crowd what had happened (and received free sandwiches for life).

Even the police officers, who had seen a lot of crazy things in their careers, found themselves talking about it over their radios:

"Hey, you hear about the miracle on Fifth?"

"Oh, yeah, my cousin was there. Said it was like

something straight outta the Bible."

"You think it's real?"

"Well, the old lady's definitely still breathing, so you tell me."

And as for the robber?

Well, he spent the night in jail—because, you know, crime—but he spent it reading a Bible for the first time in his life. And by morning he was telling his cellmate about Jesus.

In the end the little deli on Fifth Avenue wasn't just another stop for coffee and bagels anymore. It became known as "the place where miracles happened."

All because someone believed.

Because someone took Jesus at His word.

And because when you walk with God, the supernatural isn't just possible.

It's expected.

## Greater Works

When we become children of God, we don't merely receive salvation; we inherit a literal kingdom and, with it, the true ability to operate in the supernatural. This idea is not abstract; it's a biblical reality that every one of us must comprehend. You see, the Bible explicitly states that those who believe in Jesus Christ will do the works that He did—and even greater works than Him, as I've mentioned earlier (John 14:12). This is the divine mandate that was given to every believer who has ever walked this planet and those of us who are walking on it now.

Do you want to read something that I believe is extremely powerful? The millisecond that we are born again, we step into an entirely new reality. Spiritually the life we knew before is no longer there. The new reality is that we are now governed by the laws of the Spirit rather than the limitations of the flesh. In John 3:6-8 Jesus clearly explains to Nicodemus that those who are born of the Spirit operate differently from those who are born of the flesh:

> That which is born of the flesh is flesh, and that which is born of the Spirit is spirit. Do not marvel that I said to you, "You must be born again." The wind blows where it wishes, and you hear the sound of it, but cannot tell where it comes from and where it goes. So is everyone who is born of the Spirit.

What this means is that as children of God, we are no longer bound to natural constraints. The supernatural becomes our new reality. Therefore, it's unnatural for a believer not to believe in the supernatural because God Himself *is* supernatural. On top of that, because you are a spirit, it would be nonsensical for you not to believe in the spiritual realm, where 80 to 90 percent of everything in this universe happens.

You and I are given access to the power of God to perform miracles, signs, and wonders—the same as the early disciples and apostles did.

## USING THE POWER OF THE HOLY SPIRIT

After His resurrection, Jesus ordered His disciples to wait for the promise of the Father, which was the gift of the

Holy Spirit, before stepping out into ministry. He knew what the disciples didn't know at the time: Supernatural power was essential to fulfilling the Great Commission.

> But you shall receive power when the Holy Spirit has come upon you; and you shall be witnesses to Me in Jerusalem, and in all Judea and Samaria, and to the end of the earth.
> —ACTS 1:8

This power that Jesus talks about wasn't meant for the first disciples or the first church alone. It was and still is meant for every believer. To back this up, Paul even reiterates it in Romans 8:11:

> But if the Spirit of Him who raised Jesus from the dead dwells in you, He who raised Christ from the dead will also give life to your mortal bodies through His Spirit who dwells in you.

Now, if the same Spirit that raised Jesus from the dead lives in you and me, then we have true resurrection power at our fingertips! It's at our disposal! This is why supernatural manifestations are not rare occurrences for the true or deep believer; they are plainly expected.

## SUPERNATURAL ABILITIES: MESS AROUND AND FIND OUT

When our younger daughter was about three years old, she and I did everything together, as I was a stay-at-home mom and our older daughter was attending elementary school.

One sunny late-spring morning, my little one and I

drove to the dollar store around the corner in our New England town. The small town we lived in was extremely safe, and we never had an issue with anyone there.

When I pulled up to the front of the store, I parked the car, unbuckled my daughter from her car seat, took her hand, and walked her into the store. As I was skimming through items on a shelf, I noticed a man at the front of the aisle.

He was weird. Something wasn't right with him, and it was evident.

He was trying to hide at the end of the aisle so only half his body would show on my side. He began to watch my daughter and me with a weird, sinister grin on his face. He slowly moved his face back out of sight behind the shelves, and then he slowly leaned forward and grinned at us some more.

He did this over and over again.

At that moment I knew for certain that this man was under the influence of a demonic spirit. Nobody messes with my family and me, and I didn't have time for nonsense. I activated the power of God that was already inside me and prepared myself to rebuke every demon inside that man.

I moved my daughter behind me and told her to stay there. When she did, I locked eyes with the man who was trying to intimidate me and began to march forcefully toward him—like King David heading into battle.

I was ready! And when I say I was *ready*, there wasn't an ounce of fear in my bones. I was ready for a supernatural war that I knew I would win!

Right before I could open my mouth to shout "Jesus!"

the man became flustered and ran to the other side of the store.

My first thought was "Where did he go? I thought it was about to *go down!*"

What happened? Because human beings are spirits, the evil spirit in that man saw the Holy Spirit in me and knew that he didn't stand a chance. This ability has been granted to us by God, because we are His offspring and are well equipped with His granted weaponry and armor.

I'll never forget that day as long as I live. It was the demonstration of how the Holy Spirit works when we keep our armor on and use it.

The Bible outlines several supernatural abilities that we, as believers, can operate in:

- **Healing the sick.** Mark 16:17–18 says, "And these signs will follow those who believe: In My name they will cast out demons; they will speak with new tongues; they will take up serpents; and if they drink anything deadly, it will by no means hurt them; they will lay hands on the sick, and they will recover." These signs were evident in the ministries of all the apostles (Acts 3:6–8; 9:32–35).

- **Casting out demons.** In Luke 10:19, Jesus Himself declares, "Behold, I give you the authority to trample on serpents and scorpions, and over all the power of the enemy, and nothing shall by any means hurt you." You see, all believers are granted authority over demonic forces. Jesus Himself exercised this authority and demonstrated how to do so (Mark 1:23–27; Acts 16:16–18).

- **Raising the dead.** Jesus did not suggest but rather instructed His disciples in Matthew 10:8, "Heal the sick, cleanse the lepers, raise the dead, cast out demons. Freely you have received, freely give." Both Peter and Paul raised the dead (Acts 9:36–42; 20:9–12).

- **Supernatural provision.** It's no secret that God miraculously provides for His people. Jesus multiplied food (Matt. 14:13–21), and Peter found money to pay his taxes in a fish's mouth when Jesus told him specifically where to look (v. 17:27).

- **Prophecy and divine revelation.** Amos 3:7 says, "Surely the Lord GOD does nothing, unless He reveals His secret to His servants the prophets." One function of the Holy Spirit is prophetic revelation (1 Cor. 12:10; Acts 11:27–28).

- **Speaking in new tongues and interpreting the words.** The Holy Spirit grants believers the supernatural ability to speak in tongues as well as interpret what is said (Acts 2:4; 1 Cor. 14:2–5).

I'd like to touch on that last point, which unfortunately is controversial even in the church. Speaking in tongues is something God instructed people to do and then sealed the command in Scripture. For years I wondered why so many pastors and Christians hated the idea of speaking in tongues. It made no sense to me. If it's in the Bible, why challenge it? Some excuses were that it's no longer needed, it's of the devil, it scares them, or it's gibberish. Those are all insults to the Word of God.

Here's what I truly believe: The reason there's so much opposition to speaking in tongues is because the devil cannot understand what you are praying to God about when doing so. I have found praying in tongues to be one of the most effective styles of prayer. It's a discreet, encrypted message from your lips to God's ears.

The devil is a cheater, and he always wants his spies in the believer's war room. When you're speaking a language that neither he nor his minions can understand, he will deceive the whole church to make them believe it's evil and should be avoided at all costs. That way he can understand everything that comes out of your mouth. Don't underestimate the devil's influence in the church nowadays, because he does not appear to be intimidated by most of us in the Western world.

Every piece of divine inheritance mentioned in this chapter is like gold in your pockets.

# Chapter 11

# UNLOCK THE SUPERNATURAL

Vermont mornings had a way of making a person believe in God, even if they weren't trying to. The crisp air, the golden sunrise spilling over the mountains, and the way the mist curled over the valleys—it all whispered divine craftsmanship.

That's exactly what Eli thought as he stood outside his tiny log cabin, sipping a steaming mug of coffee. He took a deep breath, letting the fresh, pine-scented air fill his lungs.

"Man," he muttered, stretching his arms. "God really outdid Himself up here."

And then—*boom*! A moose. A literal, full-grown moose came crashing through the trees and skidded to a stop right in front of Eli's truck.

Now, this wasn't just any moose. This creature was *huge*. So large, in fact, that if you put a saddle on it, you could probably ride it straight into a medieval battle. It had that kind of presence. It snorted loudly and then flicked its ear as if to say, "What are *you* looking at?"

Eli sighed and rubbed his forehead. "Alright, Lord, I know You work in mysterious ways, but does it have to involve a thousand-pound animal blocking my driveway?"

Just then, from down the dirt road, came Louie—Eli's best friend, a maple syrup farmer with a thick Vermont accent and a gift for making bad decisions. Louie pulled up in his rusty blue pickup truck, rolled down the window, and squinted at the situation.

"You know," he said, taking a bite out of a maple doughnut, "this is why I usually don't leave my house before noon."

Eli waved a hand at the moose. "Do something."

Louie shrugged. "You're the preacher. Pray it away."

Eli gave him a look. "That's not how it works."

Louie took another bite and nodded at the moose. "Tell that to him."

Eli sighed, took a deep breath, and figured "Why not?" He lifted his hands toward the sky.

"Father, in the name of Jesus, I ask You to move this giant beast so I can get to church and not be late—"

Before he could finish, the moose turned around and casually walked away, as if it remembered it had better things to do.

Louie stared with his doughnut halfway to his mouth. "You for real just did that?"

Eli grinned. "Told you. Faith moves mountains. And apparently, moose."

Later that day the two of them headed to Martha's Sugar Shack, where folks were gathered for the annual Maple Festival—the biggest event in town. There were stacks of pancakes, syrup-

*Unlock the Supernatural*

tasting stations, and an old lady named Edna who was known for pouring *way* too much syrup on everything, including unsuspecting passersby.

The problem?

As soon as Eli and Louie arrived, they saw chaos.

Martha, the owner, was in full panic mode, waving her arms wildly. "The syrup! The whole batch is *ruined*!"

People gasped. Some clutched their hearts. One guy looked as if he might cry. This was Vermont. Maple syrup disasters were taken seriously here.

"What happened?" Eli asked.

Martha pointed to a giant overturned vat, syrup pooling into the dirt like some kind of sticky crime scene. "The hose broke! I lost *everything*! Months of work *gone*!"

Louie knelt by the puddle, dipped a finger into it, and tasted it like a detective. He smacked his lips. "Yeah. That's tragic."

Martha threw her hands up. "Louie, stop *tasting the evidence*!"

Eli folded his arms. "Alright. We're gonna fix this."

Martha huffed. "Unless you can make maple syrup appear out of thin air, I don't see how."

Louie nudged him. "Hey, you got that whole 'move the moose' anointing. Maybe try a syrup prayer?"

Eli rolled his eyes. "That's not—" He stopped. *Actually...*

He closed his eyes, took a deep breath, and prayed. Not for selfish reasons. Not as a show. Just pure faith.

"Lord, I know You care about the little things. And I know You provide. So I ask You—let this festival be blessed."

Nothing happened.

For a moment.

And then—

The trees started dripping.

Like, *really* dripping.

Maple sap began flowing as if someone had turned on a faucet. It was pouring out of the trees at a rate that wasn't even natural. Not only was it unnatural, but like when Jesus turned water into wine, the sap turned into syrup—bypassing the evaporation and sugaring process—right before their eyes! Within minutes, they had gathered more than they had lost.

Silence.

Then a slow clap.

Then cheers.

Martha burst into tears. "It's a miracle!"

Louie grinned. "Well, if anyone was doubting, they ain't doubting now."

Later that night, as the festival wrapped up, Eli sat back on a hay bale, exhausted but thankful. He looked at the glowing sky, the crisp mountain air filling his lungs.

"God, You really do show up in unexpected ways."

And just as he said that—

A giant stack of pancakes landed in front of him, dripping with syrup.

Louie smirked. "Martha said you eat for free for life."

Eli laughed. "You know, I think I could get used to this supernatural life."

And with that, under the Vermont sky, in the place where faith was stronger than fear, miracles were as tangible as maple syrup, and God showed up in even the smallest details. Eli took the biggest bite of his life, knowing that the best was yet to come.

## Faith—the Golden Bridge

God cares about *everything*—from replenishing lost syrup to moving moose to showing up when you least expect it. If you have faith, expect the unexpected.

The entire supernatural operates by faith. Hebrews 11:6 states, "But without faith it is impossible to please Him, for he who comes to God must believe that He is, and that He is a rewarder of those who diligently seek Him." Faith is that golden bridge between the supernatural and the natural. All miracles in the Bible were activated by faith:

- The woman with the issue of blood touched the hem of Jesus' garment, using her faith, and immediately she was healed (Mark 5:25–34).

- Blind Bartimaeus received his eyesight by faith (Mark 10:46–52).

- The centurion's servant was healed, without Jesus even being physically present, simply because of the centurion's faith (Matt. 8:5–13).

Jesus constantly emphasized utilizing your faith. He said, "For assuredly, I say to you, if you have faith as a mustard seed, you will say to this mountain, 'Move from here to there,' and it will move; and nothing will be impossible for you" (Matt. 17:20). This means that believers have the power to command situations to align with God's will.

## Nine Toes

Writing this book reminds me of 2003, the year I was married. My husband and I met when we were teenagers, and I was baffled and confused when he told me that he wanted to join the military. After 9/11, he felt it was his duty as a US citizen to defend his country, so I respected his wishes. The night before he departed for boot camp, he knelt on one knee and proposed. Of course, I said yes, and now we're past the twenty-year mark. Before we could walk down the aisle, the situation looked pretty grim for him.

Not long after boot camp, he received orders to deploy for half a year. Being in the navy was already hard on both of us, because seamen commonly are on board a ship for six months at a time.

After six months at sea, Ed was headed back home for our wedding. His last stop before his ship docked back at his base in Washington state was Hawaii. We were excited to see each other. It had been too long.

Just before he arrived home, the US declared war, and

he had to turn around and head to the Persian Gulf. He was away for a year and a half, and we had to reschedule our wedding.

When he finally made it back to Bremerton after a year of war, he had developed trench foot from his feet being wet so often while standing guard on the ship, and his pinky toe became severely infected.

Doctors advised him to stay in Washington until his foot healed, but he was determined to fly back home to Connecticut to marry me. He was on crutches, and his toe was getting worse by the day. His shipmates thought he was crazy, but he refused to seek medical attention until he reached me.

When he finally landed in Connecticut, he was sent directly to the hospital to have it examined, but the doctor didn't see him for hours because his foot was already wrapped in gauze from a clinic in Washington.

When the doctor finally unraveled the bandages, she jumped back in horror, put the rag back over his foot, and said, "We're going to have to amputate that tomorrow."

Ed was devastated, as you can imagine. It was hard to picture himself living the rest of his life with only nine toes. I told him that I'd love him anyway with all nine toes.

Something inside me knew this wasn't right. Yes, the infection went down to the bone. Yes, his open wound wasn't healing. And yes, his flesh was exposed. None of those facts could be denied, but I knew that God's report said otherwise.

So I called my pastor, and he came down to the hospital and prayed over Ed's foot. He was always there when anyone needed help, even if he didn't know the person. Ed thanked him, and he left.

My mother arrived soon after, and when she heard that Ed's toe would be amputated in less than twenty-four hours, she put her hand on his foot and declared healing in Jesus' name. There was no fear or hopelessness. She simply gave the order and made the decree.

My mother gave each of us a hug and a kiss, and then she departed. When she walked out of the room, Ed said, "I really appreciate your pastor coming out and praying for me. That was nice of him. But there was something about your mom's prayer. I felt it. I don't know what it is, but it was powerful."

The next day was the big day! The day that no one was looking forward to.

Suddenly, Ed called.

"Jenny! My toe is healing on its own!" he practically shouted. "The surgeon came in to talk to me before the operation, and when she removed the bandages to see what she would be working with, my toe had already started closing up on its own, and the infection had gone away! They don't have to cut my toe off!"

Today, we're proud to say that Ed still has all ten toes! That's the power God has equipped us with. You can move mountains and save toes, too.

## Walking in the Supernatural

Supernatural living isn't just about miracles; it's about intimacy with God. It's about having that close relationship where it's just you and Him. Jesus lived a life of prayer and communion with the Father, which serves as a great example for us. Luke 5:16 tells us that Jesus would often withdraw to lonely places to pray. This was a source of His power: closeness with the Father.

If you and I desire to move in the supernatural, it's crucial that we cultivate a deep relationship with God through all of these:

- **Prayer and fasting.** Fasting intensifies our spiritual authority (Matt. 17:21).

- **Obedience to the Holy Spirit.** God's Spirit leads us into all truth and empowers us (John 16:13; Acts 1:8).

- **Holiness and consecration.** The anointing increases when we live a pure life (2 Tim. 2:21).

- **Speaking the Word of God aloud.** God's Word carries power (Isa. 55:11).

## Experiencing Greater Works

Jesus assured us that those who believe in Him will do even greater works than He did (John 14:12). How is this possible? The Holy Spirit, that's how.

Acts 1:8 declares, "But you shall receive power when the Holy Spirit has come upon you." The early church exercised this exact power, and we are meant to walk in it as well.

Here are some examples of modern-day supernatural manifestations:

- Miraculous healings at crusades and revivals[1]

- Supernatural provision and financial miracles[2]

- Deliverance from demonic oppression[3]

- Visions, prophetic dreams, and divine encounters[4]

As children of God, we are meant to live more than ordinary lives. The supernatural should be our norm. We are seated in heavenly places with Christ (Eph. 2:6), and we have been given access to His power. Through faith, intimacy, and the guidance of the Holy Spirit, we can surely operate in miracles, signs, and wonders, bringing glory to God in advancing His Kingdom on the earth. That is our mission, and that is what we're here to accomplish.

Now is the time to rise up, walk boldly in the fullness of our identity, and demonstrate the power of God to a world in desperate need of His supernatural presence!

"For the kingdom of God is not in word but in power" (1 Cor. 4:20).

## Chapter 12

# WHAT ARE ANGELS DOING?

The day began as any other for the passengers of flight 227, bound from Miami to New York. The sun shone bright, the sky was crystal clear, and a gentle breeze swayed the palm trees at the airport. Travelers bustled through security, then stood at the gates gripping their coffee cups and boarding passes as they chattered about vacations, business trips, and weekend getaways.

Among them was Nia, a sixteen-year-old girl with a habit her friends always teased her about: She never traveled without stuffing her Bible into her purse.

"You're bringing that thing again?" her cousin had joked earlier that morning.

"Of course," Nia replied with a grin. "Never know when I'll need a word."

Before boarding, she took a quiet moment near the terminal window, staring at the bright blue sky stretching endlessly before her. She felt an odd stirring in her spirit—like an unspoken warning.

She bowed her head. "Lord, keep me and everyone on this plane safe. Let Your angels go before us. I trust You."

With that she boarded the plane, tucking herself into seat 14A, right by the window.

The first hour of the flight was peaceful. The plane hummed steadily as passengers settled in. Some dozed off, while others flipped through magazines or scrolled through their phones. Flight attendants made their rounds, offering drinks and snacks.

Nia gazed out at the endless stretch of sky, feeling an overwhelming sense of peace.

But then—*beep!* The seat belt sign flickered on.

*Ding!* The captain's voice crackled through the intercom.

"Ladies and gentlemen, this is your captain speaking. We are entering some unexpected turbulence ahead. Nothing to be alarmed about, but please remain seated with your seat belts fastened."

The plane shuddered slightly. A few passengers chuckled nervously, but most ignored it.

Then—*bam!* A sudden jolt sent drinks flying.

A loud crack of thunder roared outside, shaking the entire plane like a toy in a child's hand. The blue sky vanished, swallowed by thick, swirling black clouds. Lightning zigzagged like jagged scars across the sky.

Then the turbulence went from unsettling to violent.

Passengers screamed as the plane dipped sharply. Overhead compartments popped open, spilling luggage into the aisles. A woman clutched her baby, whispering desperate prayers. A businessman gripped his seat so tightly his knuckles turned

## What Are Angels Doing?

white. The flight attendants, usually calm and composed, looked terrified.

"Jesus." Nia gasped, her heart pounding as the plane lurched again.

The captain's voice came through the speaker again, this time strained. "Ladies and gentlemen, I apologize. We are experiencing severe turbulence. Please remain seated with your seat belts fastened."

Fear gripped the entire plane like an iron vice. The air was thick with panic and despair. But then something changed.

As Nia squeezed her eyes shut, her fear melted away. A warmth, almost tangible, filled her chest. She opened her eyes, and what she saw nearly made her gasp aloud.

Outside her window stood two massive angels, each holding a wing of the plane.

Their robes gleamed like the sun, their eyes burned with a fierce light, and their hands, although huge, held the aircraft with an almost gentle strength.

She turned her head, eyes wide.

Through her passenger side window, she saw more angels hovering at the nose of the plane, their hands stretching forward and guiding it through the storm. Down the aisles angels stood shoulder to shoulder, stationed like warriors. Each one glowed, their presence commanding peace.

At that moment she realized the plane wasn't flying on its own anymore.

Nia bolted upright. Her hands clenched around her Bible, and she spoke—not in a whisper or in fear but with authority.

"In the name of Jesus, this storm has *no* power here! The Lord is our refuge! The angels of God are with us! We will *not* be shaken!"

The flight attendants stared. The businessman who had been shaking stopped. A woman holding a picture of her grandchildren began to weep.

And then, as suddenly as it had begun, the turbulence stopped.

The roaring winds fell silent. The lightning vanished. The black clouds peeled away, revealing a calm, sunlit sky.

Passengers looked around, stunned.

The captain's voice cracked through the intercom again, this time astonished. "Ladies and gentlemen, we...we are through the storm. I don't know how, but...we are safe."

A pause.

Then cheers erupted. People clapped. Some cried. Others simply sat there, overwhelmed by what had just happened.

But Nia? She knew exactly what had happened. The angels had been there. They had held the plane in the grip of God's protection.

When they landed safely at JFK Airport, the passengers could not stop talking about it. "I swear I saw something outside," a woman muttered.

"That was...a miracle," another whispered.

The flight attendants, usually full of standard, scripted pleasantries, hugged the passengers as they exited.

The pilot—a seasoned man who had flown

for over twenty years—walked out last, shaking his head. "I don't know what kind of prayers y'all were saying back there," he said, "but something... *something* was holding that plane up."

And with that the story of flight 227 spread.

People told their friends. The passengers told their families. Some even shared it in churches, in sermons, and in testimonies across the country.

So it's important to remember that sometimes, even when everyone around you is in danger, your faith can be the key to saving the entire flight.

That day flight 227 landed safely.

Not because of the pilot's skill or the plane's technology, but because a sixteen-year-old girl named Nia believed that when she prayed, God would hear her and angels would show up.

And they did.

## THE MINISTRY OF ANGELS

Since the beginning of time God has sent angels to guide, protect, and help His children. These majestic, powerful beings operate in the spiritual realm and are usually unseen, yet their influence is undeniable. Sometimes, we get a glimpse of their presence—through miraculous rescues, divine messages, or inexplicable moments of divine intervention. Other times they work quietly in the background, often unnoticeable, ensuring we stay on the right path. The Bible is full of incredible stories that prove God's people are never alone.

The Bible makes it clear that angels have a job to do: to serve and assist those who belong to God. Hebrews 1:14

puts it plainly: "Are they not all ministering spirits sent forth to minister for those who will inherit salvation?" This means that angels aren't passive beings in heaven; they are actively working for us, keeping us safe and guiding us through life's wild twists and turns.

Let's take Daniel, for instance. The sixth chapter of the Book of Daniel tells us he was unjustly thrown into a den of lions. Now, that should have been the end of him, but God had other plans—plans that would never be forgotten, even till this day.

The next morning Daniel was still alive, and he told the king, "My God sent His angel and shut the lions' mouths, so that they have not hurt me, because I was found innocent before Him; and also, O king, I have done no wrong before you" (Dan. 6:22). The angel's intervention proved that God watches over His own.

Another great example is found in Acts 12, when Peter was locked in prison. While the church prayed for him, an angel miraculously showed up, removed his chains, and led him right past the guards to freedom. This also shows how God uses angels to deliver His children from danger and impossible situations.

## Angels in a Ditch

A couple of winters ago my mother was driving down Route 9 in Connecticut when she suddenly lost control of her car because the roads were slick with ice from an ongoing winter storm. Before she knew it, her car spun out, sliding uncontrollably from the right side of the highway— the slow lane—all the way across to the left, passing the fast lane before crashing into a deep bank of snow. Her

*What Are Angels Doing?*

wheels were buried in the snow, and no matter how much she pressed the gas, the car wouldn't budge.

Realizing she was stuck, she reached for her phone and started making calls, hoping someone could help. Despite call after call, the situation remained the same—either no one answered or they weren't close enough to reach her anytime soon. The storm had made the roads nearly impassable, and soon she accepted that she was stranded. Sitting there alone on the empty highway, she tried to figure out what to do next.

The silence was eerie. There were no other cars in sight—only the howling wind and snow swirling across the road. Then, seemingly out of nowhere, three massive, broad-shouldered men appeared, walking toward her through the thick snow. Despite the freezing cold, they didn't seem bothered or in a hurry to move through it. She barely had time to process what was happening before they surrounded her car.

What happened next was beyond anything she could have imagined. Without hesitation the three men reached down and *lifted* her car—*with her still inside*—pulling it free from the snowbank and setting it gently back onto the highway as if it weighed nothing at all. She was in complete shock. How could three men, no matter how strong, possibly lift a car so effortlessly? It defied all logic.

Overwhelmed with gratitude and astonishment, she glanced down for what felt like a second—maybe to grab her purse or phone or perhaps just to catch her breath. When she looked back up, however, *they were gone.* There were no men. No other vehicle in sight either. In fact, there were no signs that anyone had been there at all. It was as if they had vanished into thin air.

For a moment she sat there, gripping the steering wheel and trying to make sense of what had happened. Deep down she knew. This was no ordinary rescue. These weren't just three kind strangers passing by in the middle of a snowstorm.

To this day my mother insists without a shadow of a doubt that those men were *angels*—three angels who appeared out of nowhere, lifted her out of danger, and then disappeared as quickly as they had appeared. It was a moment that changed her life forever: a divine encounter she will never forget.

## Do We Have Guardian Angels?

Scripture suggests that believers are absolutely assigned guardian angels. Jesus Himself said in Matthew 18:10, "Take heed that you do not despise one of these little ones, for I say to you that in heaven their angels always see the face of My Father who is in heaven." This obviously tells us that angels are not only watching over us but also are constantly standing before God and are ready to act on His command.

Psalm 91:11–12 reinforces this: "For He shall give His angels charge over you, to keep you in all your ways. In their hands they shall bear you up, lest you dash your foot against a stone."

God's angels are always on duty, protecting and guiding us.

Most of the time angels remain invisible, but there are moments when God allows people to see them. For instance, Genesis 18 tells us that Abraham met three angels who delivered the message that Sarah would have

## What Are Angels Doing?

a son. Then 2 Kings 6 tells us that Elisha's servant was terrified of an enemy army, but when Elisha prayed, his servant's eyes were opened to see the vast army of angels surrounding them! (This is one of my personal top ten favorite stories from the Bible.)

Even today, people share testimonies of encouraging, mysterious figures who vanish after providing help. Although we don't always see them, we can be sure that God's angels are working on our behalf.

Seeing an angel is one of those experiences that stays with you, and you will never forget it—ever. It's not just about witnessing something supernatural; it's about feeling something so real and so beyond words that it changes how you think and how you view reality.

People who have seen angels often say it was completely unexpected. It seems to happen when they're at their lowest point, they're searching for answers, or sometimes when they're not searching at all. One woman who was grieving the loss of her child awoke to see a figure standing at the foot of her bed. It wasn't just the sight of it that struck her; it was the warmth that flowed from it—the overwhelming peace that filled the room. She didn't need to ask what it was. Her spirit knew.

Children seem to have an easier time seeing angels than adults do. It's as if they don't have much of a spiritual veil that separates the supernatural from the natural until they're older. They sometimes talk about "big shiny people" standing by their parents, by their beds, or outside their windows, watching over them. Some even describe figures with swords such as warriors or guards, while others say the angels just stand there—calmly and silently.

The real question isn't whether angels exist but rather how often they are around without us even knowing it. The Bible says we must always treat others kindly because we could be unknowingly entertaining angels. Could they be the stranger that we stop to help when no one else does? Do they provide the sudden feeling of peace in the middle of the storm? Are they responsible for that near miss that should've ended in disaster but somehow didn't? These are all questions we often ponder.

Maybe seeing angels isn't just about using our eyes. Have you considered that? Maybe it's about recognizing those moments when heaven touches the earth and something beyond logic steps in right when we need it the most.

The benefits of having angels protecting us stems from our identity as God's children. But the devil doesn't have anyone to protect him. He lost that advantage a long time ago. He wants you and me to look like him rather than like God. I truly do believe that there is a point where we can walk so far out of God's will that His hand can no longer rest on us (until we repent), which allows the devil to have his way in different aspects of our lives. Those may be times when an angel can't help due to a person's choices, sin, or rebellion—much like King Saul when he consulted with a medium to seek guidance about going to war against the Philistines. After that, God's hand was no longer on him. Angels were no longer fighting for him, and he and his sons gruesomely lost their lives in battle because of it.

On the upside the beautiful part is God's mercy, as it's never too late to return to Him as long as you have air in your lungs. When we step back into the covering of our loving Father and yield to repentance, His protection, His provision, and even His assigned angels will be once again positioned on our behalf.

# Chapter 13

# THE HOLY SPIRIT GIVES YOU THE UPPER HAND

Middle school is already wild enough without supernatural encounters. Among kids going through *that* awkward growth spurt, voices cracking mid-sentence, and random debates about which fast-food place has the best fries, nobody was expecting a spiritual showdown in the middle of Krystina's small Christian school cafeteria.

But it did. And it changed everything.

Welcome to Krystina's school, Holy Spirit Academy (a denominational war zone that, let's be honest, already sounds like something straight out of an intense Bible movie). But don't let the name fool you. The children at this school were not all on the same page about how Christianity worked.

Since this was a private Christian school, it had kids from every possible denomination—Pentecostals, Baptists, Catholics, Methodists, Presbyterians, and that one kid who just went to church because his grandma made him. And let me tell you, lunchtime was basically an ongoing theological debate show, where kids argued over whether

- *Veggie Tales* was biblically accurate
- It was a sin to listen to Christian rap

- The Holy Spirit still did miracles like in the Bible days, and
- Someone could *technically* be raptured in the middle of math class.

It was always hilarious because the children's arguments were usually based on whatever their parents told them.

The Baptist kids were sure that speaking in tongues was *not* a thing anymore.

The Pentecostals said, "First of all, my mom prays in tongues over my Pop-Tarts every morning."

The Catholics were arguing over whether their grandmas were right about purgatory.

The Methodists just wanted everyone to get along and be friends.

And then there was Krystina—somewhere in the middle, hoping nobody asked her too many questions.

But nothing prepared them for what happened that fateful Wednesday afternoon.

Lunch started off normally, which meant it was chaotic.

Kids were trading snacks as if they were on the trading floor at the stock market, the student who never followed the dress code was being sent to the principal's office for wearing Crocs, and someone was trying to convince the science teacher that dinosaurs are connected to the Book of Job.

And then out of nowhere, the new kid, Isaiah—who had been at the school only for about a month—stood straight up at his lunch table.

Isaiah was that type of person who was super quiet but low-key *knew things*—the type of person

## The Holy Spirit Gives You the Upper Hand

who could read you like a book simply by looking at you. The teachers called him "very observant," but everyone else was growing a little suspicious.

That's when he pointed directly at Caleb, the class clown, who was about to take a big ol' spoonful of his chocolate pudding.

"Do not eat that!" Isaiah announced.

The entire cafeteria froze.

Caleb, with his spoon halfway to his mouth, blinked. "Uh...what?"

Isaiah narrowed his eyes, sniffed the air dramatically, and said, "I don't know why, but I just *know* that pudding isn't safe."

All the students stared at him as if he had prophesied the end of the world.

Caleb squinted. "Dude, it's just pudding."

Isaiah didn't blink. "Something is *not right*."

Caleb rolled his eyes and took a big spoonful anyway.

Bad move.

Two seconds later he turned an unnatural shade of green, choked, and spat the pudding right back out onto his tray.

"Dude—what was that?" Caleb gagged.

It turns out that the pudding had expired *two months before*, and someone in the kitchen *accidentally* put it on his tray. The teachers were horrified, and the lunch ladies swarmed in to apologize.

Isaiah just sat back down, totally chill. "I told you."

The entire cafeteria lost its mind.

After that, everyone started whispering about

Isaiah's "weird ability."

The students would whisper to each other comments such as, "He knew about the pudding," "How did he know?" and "Dude, is he, like, some kind of prophet?"

At first Isaiah just shrugged it off.

But a few days later Sarah—the sweetest, most soft-spoken girl in Krystina's grade—was sitting in the chapel when she suddenly said, "I feel like someone in this room is really struggling today and needs prayer."

No big deal, right?

Until one of the eighth graders started sobbing uncontrollably in the back row because her parents were getting divorced, and she hadn't told anyone.

Then Jonah, one of the goofiest kids in the whole school, randomly prayed for his friend's twisted ankle at recess—and that friend started jumping up and down five minutes later as if nothing had ever happened to it.

At this point the whole school was *shook*.

Students were side-eyeing each other, wondering, "Who else has the gift?"

But here's the thing—it wasn't just the "special" kids. It was happening more and more to every kid there!

One student said he felt like he should pray for his mom's sickness—and she was feeling better the next day.

Another kid was led by the Holy Spirit to give his lunch to a kid who had forgotten his own. Later found out that someone had left a surprise burger

## The Holy Spirit Gives You the Upper Hand

and fries in his locker.

The history teacher said she had been struggling with a decision, and out of nowhere, a kid gave her the exact Bible verse she needed to hear.

It was as if something had been activated throughout the whole school.

One day in chapel it all came to a head.

The preacher that morning was talking about how the Holy Spirit gives us boldness, gifts, and supernatural insight—and it just felt like the air was electric.

When he asked whether anyone wanted to be filled with the Holy Spirit, people started standing. Even the skeptical kids. Even the ones who used to say, "That stuff isn't real anymore."

The next thing they knew, the students were praying for one another. Some were crying, some were laughing, and some were sitting there in awe of what was happening.

Even the teachers—who were usually strict about "no loud disruptions"—let it happen.

That's when Caleb—the same kid who had ignored Isaiah's pudding prophecy and lived to pay the price—stood and yelled, "Bro, I feel the Holy Spirit in my toes."

The entire room lost it.

Kids were laughing and crying at the same time. The Methodists were looking at the Pentecostals, admitting, "OK, y'all were *right*." The Baptists joined in, saying, "Maybe tongues aren't that weird after all."

By the end of the chapel, everyone knew something had changed. This wasn't just a random spiritual high. It wasn't just hype. It was real. And from that day on, the school was never the same.

## Who Is the Holy Spirit?

The Holy Spirit is not an "it" but a "He." He is known as the third person of the Godhead. Even though God is one being, the Holy Spirit is a person of the Holy Trinity, as we discussed earlier in this book.

Now, while angels are at work around us, God has given us an even greater gift: His Holy Spirit. Unlike angels, the Holy Spirit doesn't just help from the outside; He lives inside us while guiding, teaching, and empowering us to live the way God desires us to. In other words, angels are external, and the Holy Spirit is internal.

Before Jesus left the earth, He made an important promise to His disciples. In John 14:16–17, He said, "And I will pray the Father, and He will give you another Helper, that He may abide with you forever—the Spirit of truth, whom the world cannot receive, because it neither sees Him nor knows Him; but you know Him, for *He dwells with you and will be in you*" (emphasis added).

This promise was fulfilled at Pentecost, when the Holy Spirit came to dwell within believers (Acts 2:1–4), marking the beginning of His ongoing presence in our lives.

You know what's ironic? When the disciples began speaking in tongues in the Upper Room, people outside the building thought they were crazy or drunk. That hasn't changed, even to this day! People still see those of us who speak in heavenly tongues by the power of the Holy Spirit as weird, crazy, possessed, or drunkards.

The same Spirit who empowers us to speak in heavenly tongues also plays a key role in navigating us through life. Romans 8:14 tells us, "For as many as are led by the Spirit of God, these are sons of God." He speaks to our hearts, convicts us of sin, and helps us stay on the right path. A great explanation of this is found in Acts 16:6–7. Paul and his team were on a mission to spread the gospel wherever they went, but the Holy Spirit told them not to go to certain regions. That divine guidance redirected them to where they needed to be. When we listen to the Holy Spirit, He keeps us aligned with God's perfect plan for our lives.

## He Uses Children

Our older daughter has always been strong-willed. Along with that she has a spirit of discernment that is off the charts.

One afternoon our family decided to take a short day trip to a nearby town that we had visited a handful of times before. The town had a quaint charm to it—historic buildings, mom-and-pop shops, and a reputation for attracting tourists.

However, there was something else about it. This town was known for its deep ties to witchcraft, and the people there didn't just acknowledge it; they were proud of it.

As we strolled down the street, we came across a jewelry store that doubled as a souvenir shop. The building itself was over a hundred years old, full of history and character. We had been inside before and never thought much of it, so naturally we decided to visit again.

As soon as we reached the entrance, my daughter

yanked her hand out of mine so forcefully that it caught me off guard. She planted her feet firmly on the sidewalk and shook her head.

"I'm not going in," she said.

I turned to her, surprised. "Why?"

She looked straight at me, her expression serious and unwavering. "This place has demons. I'm not going in!"

I furrowed my brows. "Why do you say that?"

Her voice trembled slightly, and her eyes darted toward the store's entrance. I could see the tension in her body as if she were fighting off something unseen.

"Mommy, I smell it. They're in there. I'm not going in! There are demons in there!"

I reached for her hand again, trying to reassure her, but she quickly pulled away. Her little fists clenched at her sides, her feet glued to the ground. Her face twisted in distress, and tears welled up in her eyes.

"They have demons! I'm not going in there. I'm not; I'm not! I smell them! I'll wait out here—I'm not going in!"

No other store we had visited that day was an issue for her. Only that one.

Her voice had risen to the point where people passing by turned their heads. She wasn't just being stubborn; she was afraid.

At that moment I knew this wasn't merely a childish outburst. This wasn't about being strong-willed. This was discernment.

That was the Holy Spirit warning her—and us—that this was not a place we needed to be.

## HE'S A TEACHER TOO!

Jesus clearly describes the Holy Spirit as a teacher. In John 14:26, He said, "But the Helper, the Holy Spirit, whom the Father will send in My name, He will teach you all things, and bring to your remembrance all things that I said to you." This means that the Holy Spirit helps us understand the Bible and reminds us of God's truths when we need them most.

Paul further explains this concept in 1 Corinthians 2:10–12:

> For the Spirit searches all things, yes, the deep things of God. For what man knows the things of a man except the spirit of the man which is in him? Even so no one knows the things of God except the Spirit of God. Now we have received, not the spirit of the world, but the Spirit who is from God, that we might know the things that have been freely given to us by God.

This means the Holy Spirit gives us insight into God's wisdom, which we wouldn't understand on our own.

Did you know that the Holy Spirit also empowers us? I mean, who doesn't like being empowered? I know I do. In Acts 1:8, Jesus told His disciples, "But you shall receive power when the Holy Spirit has come upon you; and you shall be witnesses to Me in Jerusalem, and in all Judea and Samaria, and to the end of the earth." This power wasn't only for the early church; it's for every believer today. The Holy Spirit gives us boldness, helps us share the gospel, and strengthens us when we're weak.

Beyond power He also brings comfort. Romans 8:26

assures us that when we don't know how to pray, the Holy Spirit literally intercedes for us, giving us a boost "with groanings which cannot be uttered." In our hardest moments He is there, bringing us peace and strength.

## You're All Set

To truly experience the depth of the Holy Spirit's power, we have to stay in tune with Him. We must stay in alignment. Galatians 5:16 urges us, "I say then: Walk in the Spirit, and you shall not fulfill the lust of the flesh." When we listen to Him, we make better decisions, experience God's peace, and grow spiritually.

You see, God has given us two incredible gifts: angels to watch over us and the Holy Spirit to live within us. We have the whole package! God has taken care of the interior and the exterior. No matter what any of us may face, we are never alone. His divine help is always with us, guiding, protecting, and strengthening us every step of the way.

## Chapter 14

# YOU'RE KIND OF A BIG DEAL

Jonathan Drake held the ancient parchment to the flickering lantern light, his sharp eyes scanning its worn, cryptic markings. It smelled like dust, mystery, and just a hint of bad decisions. The edges were tattered, the ink faded, but one thing was clear—the path led to a place called the Land We Never Knew.

He smirked. That was all the invitation he needed.

"Jonathan, this is insane."

Eleanor Wade, an archaeologist who preferred logic over thrill seeking, crossed her arms as she peered at the map. "There's no record of this place. No historical documents, no legends, nothing. It's like it was erased from existence."

"Which is exactly why we need to go." Jonathan folded the map and tucked it into his leather satchel. "If history tries to hide something, it's usually worth finding."

Two pairs of eager eyes looked up at him—Max, a brainy twelve-year-old boy who could recite facts about nearly anything, and Sophie, a fearless ten-year-old girl who had the spirit of an explorer and the determination to match.

"This will be the best adventure ever," Sophie declared, swinging her backpack over her shoulder.

Max adjusted his glasses. "Statistically speaking, we have a 70 percent chance of encountering man-eating creatures, an 85 percent chance of dangerous weather conditions, and a 100 percent chance that something will go terribly wrong."

Jonathan patted him on the shoulder. "Perfect. Let's get going."

Their journey took them deep into a jungle no map had ever acknowledged. Towering trees loomed above, their massive roots twisting through the earth like frozen serpents. Exotic birds called out from unseen perches, and somewhere in the distance, something roared.

Sophie nudged Jonathan. "Was that an animal?"

Jonathan didn't break stride. "Technically, everything alive is an animal, according to my teacher."

Eleanor rolled her eyes. "That is not comforting."

They pressed on, hacking through thick vines, crossing murky streams, and dodging oversized insects that looked like they had gym memberships. It wasn't until they reached a massive stoned archway covered in strange symbols that Jonathan knew they had found something important.

Max traced the carvings. "These are warnings."

Sophie tilted her head. "Warnings like 'Turn back' or warnings like 'You're about to have a great time'?"

"More like 'Enter and suffer unspeakable horrors,'" Max muttered.

Jonathan grinned. "Sounds like we're on the right track."

A ravine stretched before them, deep and endless. A single wooden bridge swayed in the wind, its frayed ropes creaking under their own weight.

Max frowned. "I give this bridge three steps before it collapses."

Jonathan tested the first plank. It groaned in protest. "Well, that's reassuring."

Eleanor crossed her arms. "You're not actually thinking of crossing, are you?"

Jonathan stepped onto the bridge. It held.

"So far, so good," he called back.

Then, with absolute confidence, he took another step. A loud snap echoed through the jungle.

He leaped forward as the plank beneath him plummeted into the abyss.

Eleanor glared. "That was supposed to convince us?"

Sophie beamed. "This is the best day of my life."

One by one they raced across the bridge—Jonathan leading the way, Sophie laughing the entire time, Max quoting every probability of disaster, and Eleanor listing every reason this was a terrible idea.

The moment Eleanor's boots hit solid ground, the bridge collapsed behind her.

Silence.

Max adjusted his glasses. "Well, there goes our return trip."

Jonathan dusted off his hands. "Guess we'd better keep moving."

The map led them to a cave so dark that it

swallowed the light. Strange symbols lined its walls, shifting as if they were alive.

Sophie peered inside. "I love how it just screams 'bad idea.'"

Jonathan strode in without hesitation. "No turning back now."

The moment they entered, a low whispering filled the air. It wasn't wind, and it didn't echo. It was the sound of voices.

Sophie grabbed Jonathan's arm. "Tell me that's normal."

Max swallowed hard. "It's not."

As they moved deeper, the whispers grew stronger. Each of them began hearing different words—words that burrowed deep into their thoughts.

Max heard *doubt*. Sophie heard *fear*. Eleanor heard *failure*. Jonathan heard *defeat*.

The weight of it was almost unbearable.

Then Jonathan did something unexpected.

He laughed.

Eleanor blinked. "This is really not the time."

Jonathan grinned. "That's the trick. These voices are just noise. They only have power if we believe them."

The whispers shattered. The cave fell silent.

The walls shifted, revealing a hidden path.

Max adjusted his glasses. "Well, that was terrifying."

Jonathan smirked. "Onward!"

The cave walls opened to reveal a raging river—

its currents violent and unforgiving. There was no bridge and no way around it.

Eleanor groaned. "Let me guess. We build a raft?"

Jonathan was already tying vines together. "You're catching on."

With a raft made of logs, rope, and pure optimism, they set off.

Immediately chaos ensued.

The rapids tossed them like a leaf in a storm. Water crashed over them, spinning them sideways, backward, and once completely upside down.

Max clung to the raft. "We are all going to die!" he screeched.

Jonathan steered wildly. "Relax. I have a plan."

"Does it involve not drowning?!" Eleanor shouted.

Jonathan didn't answer.

Because right ahead—

There was a waterfall.

Sophie screamed. "I don't want to go out like this!"

Jonathan dug the oar into the water, fighting the current. With a last-minute swing, he yanked the raft into a side channel—mere seconds before the drop.

The raft slammed into the shore.

Silence.

Max collapsed on the ground. "I need a new family."

Jonathan patted him on the head. "That was fun, right?"

No one answered.

Finally, after days of obstacles and a host of

near-death experiences, they reached the hidden temple.

Inside, at the heart of a golden chamber, sat four identical bricks glowing softly.

Max frowned. "That's it? Bricks?"

Jonathan stepped forward, feeling an unseen force pulling him closer.

As each of them touched a brick, visions flooded their minds.

Max saw himself leading people with wisdom and courage. Sophie saw herself bringing light and joy to countless lives. Eleanor saw herself uncovering truths long buried. Jonathan saw himself walking with a purpose far greater than he had ever imagined.

Eleanor's eyes widened. "These aren't just bricks."

Jonathan exhaled. "They're pieces of the golden streets of heaven."

Silence fell over them.

Sophie whispered, "So...this was never about riches."

Jonathan nodded. "It was about who we were meant to be."

As they stood in awe, the golden light engulfed them, filling them with peace.

Max wiped his glasses. "OK. I admit it. This was worth it."

Jonathan grinned. "Told you."

They had set out looking for treasure.

Instead they had found their destiny.

## Becoming Unstoppable

Once I discovered the devil's greatest fear, I realized I could be unstoppable in the army of God. That's when it hit me: If I can be unstoppable, so can every born-again believer. I began to envision God's people finally stepping into their full power in Jesus Christ, tearing down every demonic stronghold in their path. And that's when I knew—this is our destiny: a mighty army, fully armed, well-equipped, and masters of our spiritual weaponry.

When God entrusted me with the *Deep Believer* podcast, it came at a time I least expected. I wasn't searching for it, nor was I asking—but He knew the perfect moment to place it in my hands.

When I was a little girl, I attended a church led by a powerful pastor. When he spoke, people listened. His authority and passion for the gospel captivated me, and I admired him deeply. I dreamed of one day preaching to multitudes—the same way he did.

During services I would often daydream about standing before thousands, sharing the goodness of God, and declaring the greatness of Jesus.

By the time I was an adult, I had moved to a different state. With each move I visited many churches and became a member of a few. Since my husband was in the military, traveling was a part of our life, and we met people from all walks of faith, forming strong friendships across various denominations.

However, there was one recurring pattern I noticed in my life. No matter which church we attended, I struggled to truly excel. I would become deeply involved, volunteering in areas where I knew God was calling me, yet there was always something—or someone—standing in the way. Just when I was on the verge of stepping up to the next level, a barrier would appear, preventing me from fully walking in my purpose. I longed to be as active in the church as possible while still balancing my family life, but time and time again, I felt held back.

It took me a while to pinpoint exactly when all this began because, as a child and even into my early teens, I had always received support from the church. Then something shifted.

It wasn't until we had been attending a midsized church of about four hundred people for four years that I noticed the change. One evening we went to the Wednesday night service, where a well-known prophet had been invited to speak. The atmosphere was electric. Everyone was eager to receive a personal prophecy. Excitement buzzed through the congregation as people anticipated receiving a divine word spoken over their lives.

But me? I wasn't as eager. It wasn't that I didn't believe in prophecy—I did. I already had a deep relationship with the Lord, and I felt that if God had something to tell me, He could speak to me directly, and I would listen. I didn't need a middleman to confirm what He had already placed in my spirit. Still, I sat there, observing the excitement unfold around me, unaware that this night would mark the beginning of a pivotal shift in my spiritual journey.

During the service this prophet moved through the congregation, pointing people out and "revealing" details about them—guiding them on what to do, according to what he believed God was saying. People were hanging onto his every word, eager to receive a prophecy.

Then, for some reason, in this big crowd that filled the

church, he pointed directly at me. He told me to stand up, so I did. With a serious expression, he said something along the lines of "You've experienced a lot of rejection, haven't you?"

The answer was no. I hadn't. However, at that moment, I didn't know how to say no. I didn't want to seem resistant or doubtful, so—foolishly—I said, "Yes."

After that, the rest of what he said became a blur. Nothing stuck. It was all hogwash to me. His words didn't resonate, and there was no confirmation in my spirit. That moment, which was supposed to be a divine revelation, ended up being nothing more than empty words.

The truth was that I had never struggled with rejection. I never had issues accomplishing my goals. If I set my mind to accomplish something, I almost always achieved it without any major roadblocks. Yet somehow, that one false word planted a seed—one I didn't realize at the time, but which would later begin to take root in ways I never expected. It took root because I verbally accepted it, with hundreds of people as my witnesses.

That day, when I unknowingly accepted a lie spoken over my life, everything changed. Because I agreed with words that weren't even true, the spirit of rejection took hold of me. And without realizing it, that moment became the doorway for its influence. It all started in that church—right then and there.

From that point on, every church I attended seemed to block me from excelling. No matter how involved I became and no matter how much I poured my heart into serving, I would always hit an invisible wall. Just when I was on the verge of stepping into a greater role, an unseen force would shut the door in my face. It became a relentless pattern—one I couldn't escape.

Yet, during those difficult times, I gained something invaluable. I began to recognize spiritual forces at work within the very walls of the church—forces I had never known existed. I saw firsthand how competition was on the rise and how jealousy had infiltrated nearly every congregation we joined. There was a spirit of division lurking among prayer teams and even worship teams, creating strife where unity should have flourished. And I couldn't understand why so much of this was happening to me.

I searched my heart, questioning whether I had done something wrong. I knew my motives were pure; I knew I had a humble heart and only wanted to serve God. My deepest desire was to please Him and bless as many people as Billy Graham had in his lifetime. I constantly told the Lord that I wanted my rewards to be in heaven and to do whatever His heart desired, no matter the cost. The things of this world never mattered to me. I couldn't care less about earthly recognition or success because, in the end, I knew this world is temporary. Everything it offers eventually fades away, but eternity with God lasts forever.

One day, however, everything changed.

It happened after a church service while I was speaking with a leader in the foyer. Although I can't recall exactly what she said, the moment her words left her mouth, something supernatural happened.

In an instant the Lord's voice spoke directly to my spirit, clear and unmistakable: "I've never used a church to prosper you."

The weight of those words hit me like a tidal wave. It was as if the fog I had been walking through for years suddenly lifted. I stood there, momentarily frozen, letting His words sink deep into my soul.

All this time I had been striving to excel in church after church, believing that my breakthrough, my calling, and my purpose were somehow tied to these institutions. I had thought that to walk in the fullness of what God had for me, I needed the approval, recognition, and opportunities that came from being active in a church setting. But in that moment, God shattered that belief.

He was telling me that my purpose and my prosperity—both spiritually and otherwise—was never meant to be dictated by a church or its leaders. My calling wasn't dependent on a title, a position, or a role within a congregation. It wasn't defined by how much I was allowed to serve or how far I could climb the ladder of church leadership. It was never about whether people accepted or blocked me. None of those responses had ever determined the plans God had for my life.

I had unknowingly put limitations on what God wanted to do through me, thinking it had to happen within the church walls. His words reminded me that His provision, His anointing, and His direction are far greater than any man-made structure. He was the One who called me, equipped me, and set me apart—independent of any church title or position.

At that moment years of frustration suddenly made sense. The barriers, the blockages, and the feeling of being held back weren't because I was unqualified or unworthy; it was because God had never designed my path to be dependent on a church organization. He had something different for me. Something greater.

That revelation changed everything. From that day

forward I no longer looked to a church for validation or permission to step into my calling. I knew, without a doubt, that my journey would be led by God alone, and no rejection, no man, and no system could ever stand in the way of His divine plan for my life.

For the first time in years, I felt a deep sense of peace and relief about my purpose and calling. I finally understood where God wanted me. He had heard my prayers annd seen my heart, and in His perfect timing, He brought the clarity I had been longing for.

A few weeks after that conversation, I began to witness something extraordinary. The Lord placed His mighty hand on the *Deep Believer* podcast in a way I had never seen before. Suddenly doors began to open, opportunities expanded, and the ministry's reach grew beyond anything I could have imagined.

Since then we've had the privilege of ministering to millions across the world. Thousands have surrendered their lives to Jesus Christ, faith has been ignited, and the truth about the supernatural has been unveiled like never before.

People who once doubted now believe. Miracles, signs, and wonders have followed—not just stories but real, undeniable manifestations of God's power. We've seen healings take place. Lives have been transformed. There have even been moments when literal angels played music in our presence, which was heard by thousands. These weren't coincidences or imagination; they were divine encounters that left people forever changed.

The reason I share this is simple: God has a calling that is tailor-made for you. It is a purpose so unique that no man or woman can alter, diminish, or destroy it. To you it may seem small. To others it may seem grand. But in the eyes of God, the size doesn't matter. What matters is that He has anointed you for it. Your duty is yours alone.

No task assigned by God is greater or lesser than another. Some may come with more responsibility, but that doesn't change their value in the kingdom. What truly counts is obedience: walking humbly in your calling, keeping God at the center, and remaining faithful to His voice.

Unfortunately, there may be times when others, even within the church or ministry, become envious of your anointing. It's disheartening, but it happens. Some may see you as a threat, attempting to hinder or block your progress. They may try to silence you, keep you from stepping into your purpose, or create obstacles in your path. But here's the truth: They are not fighting against you. They are fighting against God.

And no one can win that battle.

"Touch not God's anointed." We've heard it said, and it remains true. No amount of resistance from man can stop what God has ordained.

Whatever the Lord has called you to do, it will come to pass—as long as you remain obedient and steadfast in His direction. Even if it seems as if people are holding you back, remember the story of Joseph in Genesis. He faced betrayal, false accusations, and years of hardship, yet he still rose to the exact place God had destined for him.

The same goes for you. No one and nothing can stop what God has set in motion. Stay faithful, stay humble, and trust in His perfect timing.

Where God has me right now is exactly where I believe He wants me to be. Every step He has ordered, every door

He has opened, and every person He has placed in my path have led me to this moment.

One of the main reasons I felt led to interview believers from all around the world—each from different walks of life—is because I saw a deep problem within the church. The body of Christ was not only spiritually weak but also dangerously ignorant of the devil's devices.

Growing up in the Pentecostal church, I was always aware of the supernatural. I knew the power of heaven, and I knew the power of hell. I had no doubt that both were real. But over time, I came to a troubling realization: Too many Christians either didn't know this truth or flat-out refused to believe it. They dismissed the reality of spiritual warfare, thinking it was just symbolic, or they remained in denial because confronting it felt too overwhelming.

That's when I knew something had to change.

I felt a deep urgency to pull back the curtain and expose what was happening in the spiritual realm. If the church wasn't going to teach it, someone had to. That's why I invited former witches, warlocks, and sorcerers onto my show—people who had once been deep in the occult but had since surrendered their lives to Jesus Christ. My goal was simple: to uncover and dismantle the hidden schemes of the enemy by letting those who had once served him reveal his every tactic.

And let me tell you, they did not disappoint.

With firsthand knowledge they exposed the tricks, the rituals, the curses, and the manipulations they once used to keep people bound. They shared how the enemy operates, how he gains access, and most importantly how believers can close those doors and walk in total victory.

What they revealed was shocking, eye-opening, and long overdue for the church to hear.

Because the truth is that we are in a battle, whether we acknowledge it or not. And if we don't know our enemy, we will continue to lose unnecessary fights. Remember, God has already given us the victory. All we need to do is open our eyes, equip ourselves with knowledge, and take back the authority that has always been ours.

Besides the power of using the mighty and matchless name of Jesus and God Himself, the devil's fear of you walking in the full power of your authority and identity is one of your biggest advantages over him. This is a truth that every believer must grasp because the enemy thrives on deception, convincing people that they are powerless. In reality, they hold the authority that terrifies him.

Unlike people whom we are called to love, show mercy, and extend grace toward, the devil is the one and only enemy I would advise you to fully take advantage of his weakness. He is already defeated, so kick him while he's down! Refuse to give him an inch of ground in your life, your family, or your destiny. Step boldly into the authority God has given you, and align every move, every decision, and every step with the Father's divine orders.

Know whose you are in Christ. Know who you are. Walk in confidence, clothed in the armor of God, and don't just fight—win! Win! Win! Win! Because through Jesus, victory isn't just possible; it's already yours.

# A PERSONAL INVITATION FROM THE AUTHOR

IF YOU'D LIKE to be born-again and give your life to Jesus Christ today, pray this prayer with me:

*Dear Jesus, I admit that I'm a sinner and am lost without you. I'm convinced that You're my only saving grace and my only hope. No longer do I want to do life without You. I believe that You came to earth to die on the cross for my sins, rose from the dead three days later, and are coming back for me one day soon. Please come into my heart and be my Lord, Savior, and friend. In Jesus' name, amen.*

If you've prayed that prayer, please contact my publisher at pray4me@charismamedia.com so that we can send you some materials that will help you become established in your relationship with the Lord. Get yourself a Bible and read it daily and ask God to interpret every word for you. Then surround yourself with like-minded believers in Jesus Christ.

Congratulations and welcome to the family!

# NOTES

### Chapter 4

1. Blue Letter Bible, "*hêlēl*," accessed May 15, 2025, https://www.blueletterbible.org/lexicon/h1966/kjv/wlc/0-1/.
2. Blue Letter Bible, "*hêlēl*," accessed May 15, 2025, https://www.blueletterbible.org/lexicon/h1966/kjv/wlc/0-1/.

### Chapter 5

1. Kat Eschner, "Mark Twain Liked Cats Better Than People," *Smithsonian Magazine*, October 16, 2017, https://www.smithsonianmag.com/smart-news/mark-twain-liked-cats-better-people-180965265/.
2. Ron Powers, *Mark Twain: A Life* (Free Press, 2005).

### Chapter 11

1. James Lasher, "11-Year-Old Describes Miraculous Healing at Asbury Revival: 'A Genuine Touch from the Lord,'" Charisma News, March 27, 2023, https://charismanews.com/culture/11-year-old-describes-miraculous-healing-at-asbury-revival-a-genuine-touch-from-the-lord/.
2. "Financial Miracles 2021," Christ for all Nations UK, accessed June 30, 2025, https://cfan.org.uk/giving/financial-miracles-2021/.
3. Abby Trivett, "Most Powerful Moments of Kathryn Krick's Deliverance Ministry You Have to See!," Charisma News, May 21, 2025, https://mycharisma.com/propheticrevival/most-powerful-moments-of-kathryn-kricks-deliverance-ministry-you-have-to-see/.

4. James W. Goll, "James Goll: Prophetic Dream Encounters Are for You Too," Charisma News, August 21, 2017, https://mycharisma.com/spiritled-living/james-goll-prophetic-dream-encounters-are-for-you-too/.

# ABOUT THE AUTHOR

JENNIFER BAGNASCHI, A fourth-generation believer and founder of Deep Believer Ministries, hosts the internationally acclaimed *Deep Believer Show*, showcasing miracles and divine wonders. Raised by ordained ministers, Bagnaschi is known for her wisdom, humility, and deep, heartfelt interviews. Guided by her motto, "God, family, then ministry," she emphasizes Christ-centered service and humility in all she does.

Email: contact@deepbeliever.com

Website: DeepBeliever.com

Facebook: facebook.com/TheJenniferBagnaschi

Instagram: @thedeepbelievershow